The Coming
REAL ESTATE CRASH

The Coming REAL ESTATE CRASH

John Wesley English

Gray Emerson Cardiff

ARLINGTON HOUSE·PUBLISHERS
NEW ROCHELLE, NEW YORK

Book design by Pat Slesarchik

Manufactured in the United States of America
P 10 9 8 7 6 5 4 3 2

Library of Congress Cataloging in Publication Data

Cardiff, Gray Emerson.
  The coming real estate crash.

  1. Real estate investment—United States.   I. English, John Wesley,
1912-   joint author.   II. Title: Real
estate crash.   III. Title.
HD255.C27   332.6'324'0973   78-26423
ISBN 0-87000-415-8

Contents

Preface

Your home, its familiar lawn, its leaky faucet, its cluttered garage, its refinished kitchen, its well-trimmed hedges . . . your home is a money machine. For years it has been regularly depositing real dollars into the bottom line of your total worth, money that you may have already tapped for emergencies, or fun. Your home has been a good investment, maybe the best you've ever made. It has been a source of shelter and enjoyment as well as a bountiful source of cash. Can such a good thing end?

It can, and it will. With any luck it hasn't happened yet. But look around carefully. If you don't see an unusual number of houses for sale and if you aren't reading about the crash in the newspapers or hearing about it at cocktail parties, then you still have time. And if you find that people are still optimistic about real estate, and if you still hear your neighbors and coworkers talking about the killing they are making in real estate, then you are fortunate, for you are still in the midst of the most powerful and dynamic boom in American history. You will have time not only to protect yourself but to profit from the coming crash.

Most Americans today find it difficult to believe that a severe decline in real estate is imminent. Or even possible. How, they ask, can there be massive selling in real property when everyone needs a place to live? And with more people born every year, won't there always be an increasing demand for homes?

7

Is there not a shortage of land? Isn't real estate a great inflation hedge, and can't we figure that inflation is now a fact of life? Plus, aren't there great tax advantages to stimulate home buying? And think about the cost of building materials and labor . . . how can a house sell for less money than it costs to build?

These are good questions and they disclose the powerful forces that have made this the greatest of all booms. You will see why these forces have had such a stimulating effect on prices, and you will see why each of these forces is deteriorating as a reason to buy real estate. In this book, you will learn why a boom is a boom, why the crash will come, and what will happen when it does.

As professionals in financial markets, and after considerable study and research, we have concluded that the American homeowner is in real danger. When you understand this danger, you will be in a position to protect yourself and even profit from the coming real estate crash.

We begin by looking at some of the previous boom times in our nation's history along with the devastating crashes that followed them. These were times when disaster struck countless thousands of confident and optimistic people, times that look ominously similar to our situation today.

Acknowledgments

We would like to thank John Raeside, whose insight and clarity of expression proved invaluable in the preparation of this manuscript; Sarah Sutton, our perceptive illustrator; and Bonnie our typist.

We appreciate the assistance given us by the National Association of Realtors, the National Association of Home Builders, and the various local boards and realtors.

Part One

A Historical Perspective

1

The Chicago Real Estate Boom

In the year 1835 our young country was in the grip of a speculative fever. Though real estate values had been rising steadily through the early years of the decade, suddenly the price of land began to skyrocket. It was an epidemic madness that began in the eastern cities and soon spread even to the most rural areas. Americans, especially those who lived in or near cities and towns, discovered that they had seriously underestimated the value of their land. As this discovery spread, land prices soared—multiplying a hundred-, frequently even a thousand-fold. Sagacious investors, as they gazed into the future, saw the scattered cities and villages of their time growing into metropolises. Surveyors, as they took their chains and compasses out into the land, fired this vision of the glorious future and, wherever they went, people were certain that great cities would soon follow. Paper cities flourished and the fever spread.

The speculative spirit of the 1830s was not confined to any particular class of people; it seemed to extend to every walk of life. Farmers gave up their plows and became speculators in the soil they once worked. Mechanics set aside their tools and resolved to grow rich without labor. Lawyers sold their books and invested the proceeds in land. Physicians gave up their writing of prescriptions and wrote promissory notes instead. It was not unusual in those days to find day laborers discussing the mysteries of quit-claim and warranty deeds as they calculated their pending fortunes in the thousands. As people left their jobs to grab their fortunes, they left gaping holes in the nation's work force. Those who stayed on the job began to receive much more for their work. Not surprisingly, the cost of labor became exorbitant. Barbers who had for years shaved for two bits, now figured they had been working for half price. Even the simplest of services now cost much more. All of this resulted in a sharp increase in the number of consumers and a proportionate decrease in the number of producers. The inevitable result was an enormous rise in the cost of goods and services.

The sharp increase in the amount of real estate investment during the 1830s was not confined to the East. In fact, it was the young western states that most nourished speculation fever. The attention of the land investors moved from state to state—Indiana this year, Mississippi that year, Illinois another. In all of these states imaginations were running wild; but nowhere more than in Illinois, where the appetites of investors were being fed with promises of rich farms, new thriving villages, and glittering cities that were so far only paper mirages.

To the residents of Illinois the promise of wealth was everywhere. Only capital and an adequate means of transportation were needed, and both, it seemed, would soon be secured. Transportation would be provided by the proposed Illinois-Michigan Canal, and there was every reason to believe that capital would be no problem. By 1835, Illinois, like many other states, had begun chartering a multitude of banks to provide necessary development capital. Not only did the state put up a considerable sum of its own money for these banks, but the federal government was also helping out by depositing some of its funds. Investors were reassured. Money for loans flowed west—with the investors—to Chicago.

By the early 1830s there were already many sound reasons for investing in Chicago land. As a relatively unknown town, its land prices were cheap compared with eastern communities. And though the treaties were not finally signed until 1836, the Indian Wars (in which Abraham Lincoln served as a captain) had essentially banished the local Indian population. But Chicago's greatest asset by far was its incomparable location that would only be enhanced by the completion of the Illinois-Michigan Canal and a federally funded harbor. The canal would join the new Lake Michigan harbor with the Illinois River, which flows into the Mississippi at St. Louis. Upon completion of the harbor and canal, Chicago would be connected to the great inland waterway system of the developing West and would immediately become an important transportation center. Not only would the city serve the towns lying on the banks of the Illinois River and those in the state's interior, the canal would open Chicago to business from St. Louis and other great river cities.

Chicago would have business to do! Its markets would furnish a nearly inexhaustible supply of pine lumber from the forests of Michigan and Wisconsin. The richly fertile land surrounding Chicago would produce great quantities of grain. The vast prairies of the West would provide huge herds of livestock. The mines of northern Illinois, Missouri, and Wisconsin would pour their treasures into the Chicago terminus. There seemed to be no limit to the city's future. It was easy for speculators in the mid-'30s to imagine a bustling city of transportation and commerce whose influence would extend from the Atlantic seaboard to the slopes of the Rockies.

The geographical location of the new city and the prospects of its developing transportation system meshed smoothly with the prosperity of the times. Banks were loaning money eagerly and many people were learning how much money they could make through the simple use of available credit. Thus, the Chicago real estate boom.

15

Harriet Martineau visited Chicago in 1836 and left us this account of the times:

> Chicago looks raw and bare, standing on the high prairie above the lake shore. The houses appear all insignificant, and run up in various directions, without any principle at all. A friend of mine who resides there had told me that we should find the inns intolerable, at the period of the great land sales, which bring a concourse of speculators to the place. . . .
>
> I never saw a busier place than Chicago was at the time of our arrival. The streets were crowded with land speculators, hurrying from one sale to another. A negro, dressed up in scarlet, bearing a scarlet flag, and riding a white horse with housings of scarlet, announced the times of sale. At every street corner where he stopped, the crowd flocked around him; and it seemed as if some prevalent mania infected the whole people. . . . As the gentlemen of our party walked the streets, store-keepers hailed them from their doors, with offers of farms, and all manner of land-lots, advising them to speculate before the price of land rose higher. A young lawyer, of my acquaintance there, had realized five hundred dollars per day, the five preceeding days, by merely making out titles to land. Another friend had realized, in two years, ten times as much money as he had before fixed upon as a competence for life.
>
> Others, besides lawyers and speculators by trade, make a fortune in such extraordinary times. A poor man at Chicago had a preemption right to some land, for which he paid in the morning one hundred and fifty dollars. In the afternoon, he sold it to a friend of mine for five thousand dollars.*

Work on the canal did not actually begin until 1836 and it was to be another decade before the first boats would dock in the Chicago harbor, yet the anticipation was enough. In 1830 the first parcels of land sold in Chicago at auction brought only modest prices, ranging to a high of $100 for an 80-by-100-foot lot. But then the speculative rage set in. The same 80-by-100-

---

* Charles Cleaver, *Early Chicago Reminiscences* (Chicago: Fergus Printing Company, 1882), pp. 37–38.

foot parcel of land at South Water and Clark streets that sold for $100 in 1832, sold for $3,000 in 1834. One year later, the same lot brought $15,000. The *Chicago American* claimed in 1836 that one piece of land had "risen in value at the rate of 100 percent a *day* on the original cost ever since [1830], embracing a period of *five years and a half.*" The paper later observed, "Every man who owned a garden patch stood on his land and imagined himself a millionaire."

Substantial citizens as well as sharp operators became embroiled in the mania. William B. Ogden came to Chicago at the height of the speculation to check on the $100,000 real estate investment of a relative. Having surveyed the property while standing ankle deep in mud, he wrote back sadly, "You have been guilty of the grossest folly." Yet he succeeded in selling one-third of the land for the entire $100,000 purchase price. He at first dismissed the entire occurrence as sheer lunacy. "There is no such value in the land," he asserted, "and won't be for a generation." Soon, however, Mr. Ogden was to open a real estate office, build a mansion in one full square of the city's land, and in 1837 he became Chicago's first mayor.

In the mid-1830s Chicago seemed to be more a real estate lottery than a community. Feverish prices continued to rise as more and more people flocked into the booming city. Near the peak of the speculative frenzy, on July 4, 1836, ground was finally broken for the Illinois-Michigan Canal. Beneath the bunting on that happy Independence Day, talk was confident and speeches were stirring. Anyone suggesting that bust usually follows boom would probably have been lynched. Some of the most farsighted and sober of the celebrants may have been noticing ominous signs farther east where land prices had leveled and, in some areas, were actually declining. But it was difficult for even the most pessimistic to resist the feeling that Chicago would be immune as they watched the flashing spades filled with rich Illinois soil launch the city's audacious bid for greatness.

They were wrong. Though Chicago eventually would become the bustling hub of transportation and commerce that those present at the groundbreaking dreamed of so fondly, few of the celebrants would see it. Suddenly the fever broke. Joseph Balestier, in the *Annals of Chicago*, describes the scene:

The Year 1837, will ever be remembered as the era of protested notes; it was the harvest to the Notary and the Lawyer—the year of wrath to the mercantile, producing the laboring interests. Misery inscribed its name on many a face but lately radiant with high hopes; despair was stamped on many a countenance which was wont to be "wreathed in smiles." Broken fortunes, blasted hopes, aye, and blighted characters; these were the legitimate offspring of those pestilent times. The land resounded with groans of ruined men, and the sobs of defrauded women, who had entrusted their all to greedy speculators. Political events, which had hitherto favored these wild chimeras, now conspired to hasten and aggravate the impending downfall. It was a scene of woe and desolation.

It was called the Panic of 1837; it became a full-blown national depression, and Chicago was not immune. For nearly five years the wind whistled out of the pressurized national economy; real estate values plummeted, prices of goods and services fell, debtors defaulted. Land that had been purchased at $11,000 an acre in the sunny days of 1836 could not be sold for $100 an acre just four years later. Faced with enormous debts and a lean economy, the state of Illinois was forced to default. Work on the great canal came to a standstill.

Few Chicagoans escaped. By 1842 nearly every leading member of the business community had been severely compromised or ruined. For years the citizens of Chicago would remember the nightmare and, like Americans everywhere, would try to figure out why it had happened.

2

The California Real Estate Boom

To an observer in the mid- 1860s, California would have seemed a laughably implausible site for a major outbreak of speculation fever. From Monterey to the Mexican border, the vast arid land that lay between the Sierra Nevada and the Pacific seemed to be the exclusive province of the herds of cattle that grazed lazily on luxurious ranchos. These immense ranches encompassed land originally granted by Mexican and Spanish viceroys. As the territory came into the control of the United States, these titles were upheld, and in the mid-'60s the new state must have seemed tranquil and somehow timeless.

At the close of the Civil War, however, the appetite for land in the United States was once again voracious, and new, hopeful settlers moved west across the Great American Desert to the

19

coast. At first the federal government tried to preserve the big ranches, granting the westward-moving settlers parcels of land in the margins between the land-grant estates. But soon the population pressure was too great and the Spanish ranchos disappeared and were distributed to incoming settlers (known as "grangers"). By 1875 the once nearly uninhabited land was bustling with granger settlements.

For all of their enthusiasm, few of these early settlers were successful. Using farming methods that had little utility in the unique California climate, settlers moved from plot to plot looking, quite literally, for greener pastures. The problem was water, and in the early to mid-1870s it looked like the problem might be an insoluble one. The great California ranches of the Spanish land-grant days, with their huge acreage, could support a rancher's herds; but a small government grant had to be worked intensively, and such intensive land use was impossible without a steady water supply.

If you had visited a typical granger homestead in the mid-1870s, you would probably have seen the rusty remains of an ambitious beginning: a weather-scarred farmhouse, perhaps a dry, sandy creek-bed, the skeletal remains of a stable covered partially with old straw. And if you had found settlers living on the land, they, like thousands of their neighbors, would be studies in despair as they talked of their struggles with the weather, the rock-hard soil, and marauding wildcats, rabbits, quail, crows, and jays.

There was land in California. Land was available for little more than land-office fees. But as the land and the years took their toll on the once-hopeful grangers, there were few new buyers.

Thus 1875. Ten years later the picture was much different. If you had returned to the formerly forlorn homestead you would likely have found it much changed. The once barren hills might now be covered with fruit trees. Corn and hay might now well cover the flatlands. A closer look would reveal the source of this miracle. Above the stream that had been dusty and dry before, one could now find a dam, a pond, and a rudimentary irrigation system.

Californians were realizing their dependence upon water engineering. By the mid-1880s, crude earthwork irrigation systems had become the precursors of the giant dams and aqueducts of our time. And they brought the same results. With the water came crops and money and settlements, churches, schools, and homes. Standing on what had been worthless wasteland a decade earlier, you would have found, in 1885, a desert in bloom. Land that could, in 1875, be taken for the asking was now worth $200 an acre.

The decade had also brought a revolution in the quality of California fruit. Persistent experimentation in cultivation techniques had begun to produce fruit trees that were suited to a dry climate, while producing large yields of superior quality fruit.

The California climate, once the scourge of the struggling granger, became one of the state's greatest attractions as farming techniques and irrigation technology were developed. Prior to 1885 Pullman cars transported only winter tourists, who arrived in the fall and left in the spring with the regularity of Canadian geese. As settlement increased, however, tourists discovered the comfortable California climate, and soon the trains were running year-round. Many of these wealthy travelers from the East found the state to their liking and decided to stay. As eastern newspapers published ever more alluring descriptions of the balmy western paradise, greater numbers of settlers arrived to buy land that couldn't be opened fast enough.

Frequently these new settlers elected to stay in the small, but fast-growing, towns of Los Angeles and San Diego. By 1886 it was not unusual to see an event on the streets of Los Angeles that resembled a midwestern county fair: bands playing, food piled in abundance on picnic tables, people milling and talking. It would not be a fair, however, but the opening of a new residential development. In the center of the crowd would be a map marked off in a puzzle of lots, and a podium for the auctioneer. In early 1886 these lots would have sold for $185 to $200 an acre, but soon the prices escalated sharply. Population in San Diego during the historic summer of 1886 increased at a rate of 500 a month, while in Los Angeles the growth rate mushroomed to 1,000 newcomers a month.

During that summer, with money changing hands so rapidly, there were soon many wealthy eastern visitors playing the booming market. They brought huge sums with them, and the newly founded southern California banking system began to fill with their deposits.

Paradoxically, it was not the region's rich agricultural land that was being bartered, but small 10- and 20-acre tracts—parcels of land too small for profitable cultivation. People who once might have bought land for cultivation and improvement were now buying city lots, speculating on price rise alone. Even people who eventually hoped to invest in agricultural land entered into the city real estate market first, hoping to dramatically increase their capital.

The fall of 1886 saw the rate of migration into southern California increase still further, aided by a price war between the region's two railroads, the Santa Fe and the Southern Pacific. As new residents arrived by the trainful with their bulging purses, the real estate market reached a sort of critical mass. The tone of real estate trading began to change.

With the fever burning stronger, credit buying became common. In the spring of 1887, highly leveraged speculative money had been spent to purchase land far from the centers of the developing cities. Down payments for this land ranged from 25 percent to 33 percent. Banks, filled with new deposits, had money to lend and were encouraging such speculation. In that spring, lots were selling by the 25-foot parcel, and two of these lots were selling for more than one 50-foot lot. During the summer months of 1887, thousands of acres were platted into these 25-foot lots and sold to people who had no reason even to lay eyes on the land they had purchased. In midsummer 1887, a 60-day turnover was bringing up to $10,000 an acre. Fortunes were being made so quickly that buyers, standing in line all night for the chance to buy a slice of a paper city, might be persuaded to sell their places for up to $1,000.

Meanwhile, the population of southern California cities continued to swell. Los Angeles was gaining residents at the rate of 2,000 people a month, while San Diego was registering an increase of 1,000 a month. In the summer and fall of 1887 some long-term California residents began to chafe at this invasion. One has left his reaction:

> What? Jeeeerusalem! Shall I who have lived on beans
> and peppers and rustled clams these many years on

the salt-sea shore so as to hold my lots, now see some rich old duffer from the east get still richer at my expense?

Shall I, who have chewed jerky these many years and never could afford to eat a decent beef-steak out of my own cattle, now see the stranger drinking champagne out of the profits of the land I sold him at a sacrifice because I was fool enough to think he was paying me more than I thought it was worth?

Shall I, who have for years tried to sell those blasted lots for enough to pay the fare for myself and family out of the town, and couldn't do it, now get left with only a few thousand dollars?

Not much! I haven't skinned dead cattle to save their hides in dry years, and drunk mescal instead of good whiskey, for nothing. We never knew what the cussed land was worth until outsiders found it out, and now we are green enough to let them make all the money out of it.*

So, many natives began to climb on the bandwagon, buying back, at 5 to 15 times the price, land they had sold only a year before.

In the fall of 1887 southern California was at the peak of a major real estate boom, but like the unhappy residents of Chicago 50 years earlier, no one saw it as a boom. They saw it as destiny and buttressed their optimism with thousands of glowing arguments. Indeed, the conditions for growth in southern California seemed as dynamic as they had seemed to the Chicagoans who had toasted the first step in the construction of the great canal. The land, with its new irrigation systems, was rich and bountiful. The climate was superb. The population had skyrocketed and was still increasing with every westbound train. Agriculture was finally flourishing, and a market for California produce was now firmly established.

But this thinking, coming from the peak of speculation fever, stubbornly ignored the fact that prices had been confidently anticipating all of this growth potential for years. By mid-1887 there were enough town lots in private hands to accommodate a full 10-years' growth, even if the exponential population increases were to continue.

* Theodore S. Van Dyke, *Millionaires of a Day* (Fords, Howard Hulbert, 1890).

More important, the highly leveraged paper cities created during the boom, floating as they were on a flood tide of debt, could not have possibly been paid for in full. There simply was not enough money in circulation west of the Mississippi. The most obvious oversight had to do with the land itself. There simply was too much of it—more than enough good land existed in southern California to break any market.

And break it did. By January 1888, activity in the real estate market was at a standstill. Though this was viewed as a temporary lull caused by the upcoming presidential election, boomsters found themselves switching from French champagne to California Riesling. By April, with a thousand times more real estate on the market than could be used for legitimate business, prices were dropping weekly. During the summer the sale of any but the productive land that lay outside the towns was next to impossible, even at greatly reduced prices. The crash continued into 1889, even as the buildings started during the boom were being finished. Indeed, new houses and stores were rising in the major cities, the countryside was filling with more settlers than ever before, and southern California was selling more produce at higher prices than at any previous time in its history. Yet land prices collapsed to one-fourth and less of their previous levels. The trains carried home thousands of broken people. The great California land boom had ended.

"We were," wrote a despondent Californian, "a lot of very ordinary toads whirled up by a cyclone until we thought we were eagles, sailing with our own wings in the topmost dome of heaven."*

* *Ibid.*

3

The Florida
Real Estate Boom

Like the speculative epidemics that raged in Chicago and
southern California, the Florida real estate boom began gradually. And like the previous land price explosions, a foundation
of good sense lay beneath the apparent madness.

In the years preceding the first boom year, 1924, there were
many good reasons for investing in Florida land. The foremost
reason was, of course, the climate. As the nation's only semitropical state, Florida had an irresistible attraction for the

snowbound residents of the Northeast and Midwest. Moreover, Florida was accessible, and growing more so with each passing year. There had been a rail link between Florida and the great northern cities since 1896, and with the sharply increased number of private automobiles and the completion of the Dixie Highway, the Sunshine State seemed closer than ever. As America slid into the Roaring Twenties, more and more families could be seen on the Dixie Highway, touring southward in their flivvers from auto-camp to auto-camp in search of sunny leisure.

The '20s were also the years of the so-called Coolidge Prosperity, a state of mind that persuaded Americans from every walk of life that they would soon be able to buy a house and the good life. Florida, with its clean air, balmy nights, and sandy beaches seemed the best of the good life. As in most prosperous times, there was a widespread, though only half-acknowledged, revolt against the very urbanization and industrialization that were responsible for the prosperity. People yearned to leave the routine standardization and smoky urban congestion upon which the Coolidge Prosperity was based. They wanted to get away into a never-never land that combined American sport and comfort with Old World glamor—a Venice with bathtubs and electric iceboxes, a Seville with 18-hole golf courses.

Prohibition added to Florida's luster; only a few sea miles away were Bimini, Cuba, and Nassau, where there was no Prohibition. Even Floridians who never visited these islands felt more exotic by association.

The land and climate of Florida did more than fuel the dreams of urban America. It also produced a rich agricultural bounty. Its long growing season and semitropical rainfall made Florida a major producer of fruits and vegetables. Rich soil at relatively cheap prices made Florida land a good investment for farmers.

With all these factors in Florida's favor, it is not difficult to see why the state sparked the interest of investors. Farmers and developers began to acquire land at just a few dollars an acre. Farmers saw the land as a path to a good living at a modest cost. Developers foresaw a need for vacation residences and set about to develop the land, trusting that they would receive a good return on their investment. Other people saw Florida as

26

a good place to live, and simply moved south to enjoy the environment. And so the rate of growth in Florida began to rise.

America had been in the grip of a business depression from 1919 to 1921. But, as the depression eased, subtle changes began to affect the Florida economy. More sophisticated money began to arrive in the state, and these developers promoted the sale of Florida land more aggressively. By 1924 this sales strategy began to pay off. Americans began to take notice of Florida and its quickening real estate market. By 1925 the boom was running at full force, fueled by a huge wave of speculation.

It is interesting to try to capture the mood of the 1925 Florida boom. Fortunately we have the account of T. H. Weigall, a British journalist who wrote in 1931 about the whole crazy era. Weigall arrived in New York City from London on August 12, 1925. It was his first trip to the United States. Walking through Manhattan, he was fascinated with advertisements and billboards promoting Florida.

If he needed further encouragement, he found it that night at the Ziegfeld Follies. He heard a singer croon a song about the delights of the "Bam-Bam-Bammy Shore," then saw a lime-lit backdrop with a legend that read, "Biscayne Bay, Florida— The Eternal Summer Paradise Where Work Is No More." This was followed by Will Rogers telling stories of the people who were daily making their fortunes in Florida.

Leaving the theater, Weigall soon saw a great illuminated sky-sign at the corner of Fifth Avenue and 42nd Street, showing a tropical paradise with brightly lit castles towering into a starry sky while, in the foreground, ladies and gallants drifted lazily in spacious gondolas. A few blocks more brought a notice in the window of a real estate office which read: "One good investment beats a lifetime of toil." There was a reference to the Florida Land Boom underneath as well as an authenticated story of a young man who had made $500,000 in four weeks by his "judicious judgement of land values." "Say, YOU can do what George Cusack, Jr. did!" read the ad.

The very next morning, Weigall was at the offices of the Clyde Steamship Company, where he found that passage could not be secured for a month. His next stop was the Pennsylvania Railroad, where he was able to book space for the next day's

27

train. The 1,500-mile journey on the Southern Express was hot and crowded. The train was jammed with Florida boomsters. They came from many places and had little money, but they were all on their way to make their fortunes in the magic state of Florida.

Weigall's story is, of course, not unusual. The accompanying graphs illustrate how by 1925 people from all over the country were flocking south to Florida with their money. Not only were railroads overcrowded, but steamships were booked solid for weeks in advance, and the Dixie Highway was something to behold. Gertrude Mathews Shelby, writing in the January 1926 issue of *Harper's Monthly*, described the way the Dixie Highway looked in the summer of 1925:

> Concealing their destination from neighbors who might think them crazy, [people] climbed into the flivver, or big car, or truck, and stole rapidly down to Florida.
> . . . They found themselves in the midst of the mightiest and swiftest popular migration of history—a migration like the pilgrimage of army ants or the seasonal flight of myriads of blackbirds. From everywhere came the land seekers, the profit seekers. Automobiles moved along the eighteen foot wide Dixie Highway, the main artery of Eastcoast traffic, in a dense, struggling stream. Immense busses bearing subdivision names rumbled down loaded with "prospects" from Mobile, Atlanta, Columbia or from Northern steamers discharging at Jacksonville. A broken down truck one day stopped a friend of mine in line. The license plates were from eighteen different states, from Massachusetts to Oregon. Most of the cars brimmed over with mother, father, grandmother, several children and the dog, enticed by three years of insidious publicity about the miracles of Florida land values.

Estimates of the number of visitors to Florida in 1925 range from three to ten million. Most of these people were involved in buying and selling real estate, and some of them were making big money. The binder system, which allowed the buyer to put down only 10 percent of the value of the real estate, propelled modest amounts of money into huge profits. The first

PASSENGER EARNINGS
FLORIDA AND EAST COAST RAILWAY

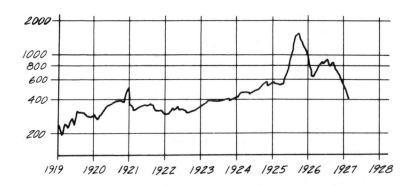

LOANS AND DEPOSITS
NATIONAL BANKS IN FLORIDA

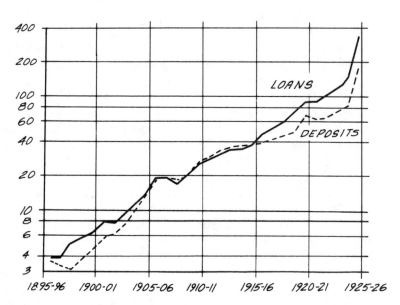

SOURCE: THE JOURNAL OF LAND & PUBLIC UTILITY

29

genuine installment, of usually 25 percent of the purchase price, was not due until title to the property had cleared, and with congestion in the law offices in the summer of 1925, a four-to-six-week delay could be expected.

Thus, under this system, immense fortunes could be made in a short time. As long as land values were rising rapidly it could be done from practically nothing. A man or woman arriving in Florida with total capital of $1,000 would buy property for $10,000 and sell it the following week for $15,000, provided a return of $3,500 after deducting the broker's 10 percent commission. With this sum in hand, or belonging to them on paper, they might buy other property for $35,000, and so on indefinitely. This procedure was not only possible but was, actually, in the later months, the normal way of doing business.

Another way of raising capital was to wait in line to purchase lots in the new subdivision openings. Those who were early in the long lines were guaranteed a profit immediately if they wanted to take it. In fact, places in line could be sold to other eager buyers, and not one cent of capital was actually necessary for place-in-line sellers to start their pyramid.

The price rises were phenomenal! A not uncommon example found in the city records of Miami shows a plot of land that changed hands in 1914 for $1,500, and in 1926 for $1,500,000—an increase of 1,000 times. People who had owned land for years saw their property go from, say, $10,000 to $50,000. They sold, only months later to see the same property selling for $100,000. This phenomenon caused people to jump into the market no matter what the price and no matter where the real estate was in order not to be left out.

The builders were also having a heyday. A small bungalow that cost $7,000 to build could be sold *before being built* for $20,000 or higher. The banks, of course, did quite well. They had huge deposits from which to loan, and the more money they loaned to the buyers at their doors, the more money they made. Cities and builders themselves were issuing real estate bonds paying 8 percent to make sure there would be enough available money to develop the land.

This mania prevailed throughout 1925 and into 1926. It seems impossible that people could pay prices so out of line with any conceivable practical value. But those who held back were thought ignorant.

At the peak of its frenzy in the late summer of 1925, the boom began to falter—predictably enough, though few knew it at the time. By early 1926 some observers were noticing that the influx of new buyers was smaller than expected. This led to some subtle changes in the market. These astute observers were also noticing that they and others were having a bit more trouble selling their binders and property. The market was moving slower and worry began to spread. To allay these worries, the government issued statements from its analysts describing the slowdown as a healthy breathing spell that would allow the boom to continue for years. Few Floridians felt like arguing. Gertrude Mathews Shelby claims to have asked more than 90 people during these months about how long the boom would last. The nearly universal answer was four to five years. Indeed, as late as October of 1926, after two hurricanes had battered the state and its land prices, worsening an already serious situation, the *Wall Street Journal* was still stubbornly insisting that the boom would continue.

But the *Journal's* words were shouted into a gale. The crash had, by that fall, been obvious for months. People who held binders had been forced into default. There were many cases when, through a series of defaults, land—blighted with half-completed developments—came back to its original owner. These hapless owners often found that accumulated taxes and assessments on their reacquired property amounted to more cash than was generated in the original sale. Nearly everyone who had any property interests in Florida after the market peaked in mid-1925 was wiped out. Many banks failed and, by 1930, when the general business depression set in, no fewer than 26 Florida cities had gone into default.

Bank Clearings for Miami

1925	$1,066,528,000
1926	632,867,000
1927	260,039,000
1928	143,364,000
1929	142,316,000

Bank clearings for Miami, which had climbed to over a billion dollars in 1925, accelerated downhill. It is interesting to note that the years shown above were the very years when, elsewhere in the country, prosperity was triumphant and was reflected in rising stock prices rather than real estate.

After the Florida hurricanes of late 1926, real estate investment lost its luster for most people. Yet the national speculative
fever that had turned their eyes and dollars to the Florida Gold
Coast in 1925 was not chilled; it was merely checked.

Florida houselots were a bad bet? Very well then, said the
public, still enthralled by the radiant possibilities of Coolidge
Prosperity, what else is there? Before long, a new wave of popular investment was accumulating momentum, not in real estate
this time, but in something quite different. The focus of attention shifted from Flagler Street in Miami to Broad & Wall streets
in New York, for the Great Bull Market was getting under way.

4

The Stock Market Boom of the Roaring Twenties

In 1924, Henry Ford produced his ten-millionth auto, a Model T that sold for $290. This car was quickly perceived as the emblem of a prosperous time. Coolidge was in the White House. Economic activity was gaining momentum, and as real personal income steadily rose, Americans found their memories of the 1920 depression fading. Confidence grew. Business was flourishing and finally even Wall Street began to reflect the national prosperity. For 10 years, the Dow Jones Industrial Average had fluctuated within a range of 70 to 100, but in 1924 the Dow passed 125, inaugurating the Great Bull Market of the Roaring Twenties.

Throughout 1925, stocks continued their slow but inexorable rise, finishing the year at 155. In 1926 the pace of events picked up. The first quarter began with an abrupt decline, and though the market proved resilient, recovering its lost ground, another sharp decline hit in October as a hurricane extinguished the last sizzling embers of the Florida Land Boom. Again the market was able to recover, but it finished the year essentially unchanged.

It had been a skittish, nervous year, but the Bull Market was not to be denied. The collapse of the Florida Land Boom had shaken Wall Street slightly, but it was ultimately to benefit. As investors became less confident of the safety of real estate, their interest switched to stocks. And there was still plenty of money to invest, which the government continued to ensure by increasing the money supply (a decision soon to be seen as a grave error). With this greatly expanded pool of money sloshing through the economy, margin requirements were reduced until they were razor thin—often only 10 to 20 percent of market value was required for these loans. So it was a well-fed bull market that trotted through 1927, finishing at 194—the Dow up a solid 25 percent.

Perhaps the first signs of the dark future that lay ahead could be glimpsed in the spring of 1928. Not that there wasn't every reason for optimism. The nation was at peace. Business was booming. The Coolidge administration continued to pledge that only the most minimal taxes would be charged against corporate earnings, which were escalating so rapidly that even the most conservative of analysts believed stock prices had a long way to go to catch up. The American public clearly believed that price increases were a virtual certainty. Still, for those who looked closely, the dark signs were there. By the spring of 1928, the stately bull market of the mid '20s had become a stampede. The speculative orgy had begun.

The spring advance in 1928 showed a change in the character of the market. Gone were the days of steady, reliable gains. Suddenly the market was charging ahead wildly, in quantum leaps. On March 12, for instance, a premier growth stock called

Radio (now RCA) jumped a full $18 a share, only to open another $22 higher when trading started the next morning. A record volume of 3,875,910 shares traded was registered on March 12, but that record was to last barely two weeks. On March 27, the ticker tape ran two hours late as an astonishing five million shares changed hands.

Nineteen twenty-eight was a presidential election year. Wall Street's attention was focused on the contest between Herbert Hoover and Al Smith, believing that the election of Hoover would mean continued prosperity. Hoover won by a landslide and the market responded with a boiling rally. Daily trading volumes were now exceeding a previously unprecedented six million shares a day.

Nineteen twenty-eight was a good year indeed. At year's end the Dow was at the 300 level—up over 50 percent for the year. Even larger gains were registered by individual issues: Montgomery Ward jumped from 117 to 440 dollars a share; Du Pont soared from 310 to 525; and Radio advanced from 85 to an incredible 420 dollars a share. The huge growth in stock prices was financed by an equally large jump in loan financing. In just a few months in early 1926, margin loans (money borrowed on stocks to buy stocks) increased from $1.5 billion to $2.5 billion. Loans outstanding jumped another billion in 1927, and in 1928 they soared to $6 billion. Since stocks are normally purchased on a cash basis, the volume of margin loans outstanding is a measure of speculative activity. As speculation increases, so does the demand for loans used to finance the speculation.

Since a 5 percent return on a secure investment was seen as normal in this period, the interest rates on margin loans also began at 5 percent. But, lashed by the heavy demand for stock financing, the interest rates soon began to rise. At the end of 1928, interest rates on margin loans had climbed to a lofty 12 percent. Even at this level, demand for loans was still insatiable. Banks could borrow money from the Federal Reserve at 5 percent and put the same money on the margin-loan market at 12 percent. Many corporate heads found it more profitable to place their capital on the margin loan market than it was to invest it in their own corporations. Demand continued to accelerate and interest rates continued to rise, peaking in March of 1929 at 20 percent.

The feverish pace of stock advances continued unabated into 1929. At that time Wall Street analysts were fearing that the country might actually be running out of common stock. As extraordinary as this sounds to us, at the time it seemed a significant crisis. Some stock issues were in such demand that they had a scarcity value. Some of these issues, it was feared, soon would not appear on the market at any price.

Nonetheless, during the summer months of 1929 the market sizzled. Margin loans continued to expand at a rate of $400 million a month. The June issue of *American Magazine* echoed the universal euphoria: "The economic condition of the world seems on the verge of a great leap forward." Banks, preparing for this great leap, had already formed subsidiary brokerage houses. They had every reason to support the public enthusiasm, as it was a booming source for their balance sheets as well. The "Boom," it seemed, would last indefinitely.

On September 3, 1929, the volume stood at 4,438,910 shares and the market appeared strong. The Dow stood at 381. Radio closed at $505 a share, AT&T at 304, GE at 396, and U.S. Steel at 262. The previous week, margin loans had expanded another $137 million. As trading closed that day, brokers, bankers, corporation executives and individual stockholders all had a sense of optimism. More stocks were owned by more people than ever before. What they were seeing was not a boom but a "new era of prosperity." Thousands had made fortunes in the stock market and everyone assumed that the future would be as bright as the past. Money that was made from stocks was being invested in more stocks. As a result, stock prices continued to rise, guaranteeing more profits for investment in still more stocks. Stocks were going up because they were going up. As the traders left the floor on that early September afternoon they may have been thinking of this spiral of fortune. If so, it would be the last time. As the trading floor quieted and the ticker tape stopped, Wall Street had seen the last of the Great Bull Market of the Roaring Twenties.

The market hit its first "air pocket" on September 5. Severe damage was done to most stocks. That same day, economist Roger Babson, speaking before his annual National Business Conference, observed: "Sooner or later a crash is coming and it may be terrific."* He predicted that what had happened in Florida would now happen on Wall Street. The Dow, thought Babson, would most likely decline 60 to 80 points. The September issue of the *Commercial and Financial Chronicle* quoted him as saying, "Factories will be shut down . . . men will be thrown out of work . . . the vicious cycle will get in full swing and the result will be a serious business depression."

Despite its uncanny accuracy, this prediction was, of course, immediately ridiculed. The brokerage house of Hornblower and Weeks reassured its customers with an ad in the *Wall Street Journal*: "We will not be stampeded into selling stocks because of the gratuitous forecasts of a well-known statistician."† Babson was thus dismissed as a technician with his charts and mumbo-jumbo configurations.

The decline on Thursday, September 5, became known as the Babson Break. A refreshing rally the next day seemed to indicate that the sharp September 5 decline was nothing but a temporary aberration. But such thinking was soon proved wishful. For more than a month, the market seesawed nervously. The trend continued to be down.

On Monday, October 21, the ticker tape was again lagging far behind the volume of trade. By noon it was an hour late, and it was to remain so until the close. Usually the late tape was a good sign, giving investors a chance to catch their breaths after the exchange closed as they waited to find out how rich they had become. On this day, however, the market was again plunging—falling all morning, only to be rescued by an afternoon rally. The market actually closed higher that day, but the sharp morning decline and the lagging ticker had brought much anxiety. Monday was followed with a fragile gain on Tuesday, and Wednesday's opening seemed calm. But then lightning struck. A heavy sell-off near the close sent the market into a precipitous decline. Prominent individual issues plunged by as much as $15 to $46 a share. To further complicate the confusing situation, an ice storm hit the Midwest, hampering communications.

* John Kenneth Galbraith, *The Great Crash* (Boston: Houghton Mifflin, 1954).
† *Ibid.*

On Thursday, October 24, the crash started in earnest. On that day an astonishing 12,900,000 shares changed hands. But even more phenomenal than the volume was the extent of the collapse of prices. Since the market was highly leveraged with margin loans, the drop was sufficient enough to wipe out the equity of thousands. Holders of margin loans were required to put up cash to compensate for the lowered value of their stock holdings, or else their stock would be automatically sold. There was little response to these "maintenance calls," and big blocks of stock were sold. This selling provoked still more selling and the decline began to feed on itself in a mirror image of the self-fueling advances of the past. By 12:30 P.M., due to the near riot conditions on the floor, the visitors' gallery was closed to the public. Among the departing visitors was a former chancellor of the British exchequer, Winston Churchill.

As word of the bizarre events on Wall Street spread, a grumbling mob began to gather outside the exchange, prompting Police Commissioner Grover to dispatch a detail of police to the scene. As the mob milled outside on the street, prominent bankers assembled in the office of J. P. Morgan to discuss their strategy. In a move to try to lend organized support to the market, they sent Richard Whitney—vice president of the New York Stock Exchange and its highest ranking officer in the absence of vacationing President E. H. H. Simmons—to the post on the trading floor where U.S. Steel was being traded. The tall, aristocratic executive confidently bid for 10,000 shares at $205 a share. His bid was several points higher than the prevailing bids. He moved around the floor and repeated this practice with other stocks, hoping that the tactic would help to stabilize the market. It did. The market rallied sharply near the close of trading, and the day ended with the market down only 6.38 points after having trailed by as much as 33.5 points earlier.

For the next two days, it appeared that the bankers' strategy had worked. Friday and Saturday saw trading volumes falling to just half of Thursday's frantic pace. A Boston investment trust ran an ad in the *Wall Street Journal* urging restraint: "S T E A D Y Everybody! Calm thinking is in order. Heed the words of America's greatest bankers."

But it was all in vain. The bankers' assurances were not

trusted. On Monday, October 28, the market again dropped violently on a volume of some 9.25 million shares. Losses in individual issues were immense: GE down $48 a share, Westinghouse down 34, AT&T down 24, and U.S. Steel down 18. Lights burned late again that night in brokerage houses throughout the country as brokers and clerks attempted to assemble the results of a devastating day.

Tuesday, October 29, 1929—Black Tuesday—brought what still stands as Wall Street's greatest disaster. The volume soared to an astronomical 16,410,030 shares. Stocks were sold into a virtual vacuum. The Dow plunged 30.5 points, which would be the equivalent of a 100-point drop from a Dow level of 900. Thousands were ruined as the tool of leverage became a sword, hacking at equity until there was nothing left.

For the next three years the market continued its ruthless slide, stopping only periodically to entice bottom-guessers along the way. Below is a table of some of the premier stocks of the day:

	March 3, 1928	September 3, 1929	July 8, 1932
Air Reduction	60	216	32
Anaconda	54	162	4
Burroughs	31	73	7
J. I. Chase	256	350	23
Du Pont	98	215	22
General Electric	129	396	28
General Motors	140	182	8
Montgomery Ward	134	467	4
RCA	95	505	18
U.S. Steel	140	262	22
Westinghouse	92	313	16

On July 10, 1932, the Dow Jones Industrial Average finally bottomed at 41.22, down from its peak of 381.17 in September 1929. It would be 22 long years, 1954, before the Dow Jones Industrials would see that level again.

5

The Apartment Boom

If the normal state of the American economy in the century that led up to the definitive crash of 1929 seemed to be a tumultuous cycle of booms and busts, the years following the Second World War seemed the opposite. From 1947 through 1967, the economy generally followed a pattern of steady, calm expansion and growth. In the two decades that followed the war, the Dow Jones Industrial Average climbed more than 500 percent. This consistent growth was coupled with an inflation rate that averaged less than 2 percent a year. America was maturing into its new role as the world's premier industrial power, and in the halcyon days of our postwar prosperity, the frantic speculative epidemics that had struck Chicago, southern California, Florida, and Wall Street seemed but faraway historical relics—the bumptuous adolescence of an economy now fully adult. Yet, commencing in 1967 financial analysts began to notice that in one sector of the economy there was a re-emergence of an old but familiar pattern. It was to last until 1972, and we will call it the Apartment Boom.

You have probably never heard of the Apartment Boom. Though huge sums of money were made and then lost during those years, the boom has never been widely publicized. Neither has the crash that followed it. This is because the people who speculated on the boom in the prices of rental property, watched the action from the boardrooms of most of America's largest banks and financial houses—institutions that do not frequently publicize their misfortunes. Still, the Apartment Boom of the late '60s and early '70s deserves our attention, for the fundamental forces behind it are still at work in today's superheated real estate market.

The roots of the explosion of rental property prices that was felt around the nation in the late '60s penetrate back nearly two decades—back to the joyous days at the end of the Second World War when America watched the dawning of the first new "era of prosperity" since the early 1920s. In railroad depots and airports around the country, Americans were reunited and eager to begin the process of claiming long-deferred dreams. The harsh realities of depression and war had tempered our vision of "the good life." Visions of quick fortunes were replaced with more sober visions of homes in good repair and incomes adequate to raise a family. America's new and powerful position in the world meant a rapidly expanded industrial base, jobs and prosperity. The recovery of the stock market indicated the degree of this prosperity. But Americans were not only investing in stocks. We were also investing in ourselves.

From 1945 through 1947 the United States witnessed a new boom that reached almost epic proportions, but it was a boom quite different from those we have chronicled so far; it was charted not on the financial pages but on cradle rolls and in maternity wards. The immediate postwar years saw an extraor-

41

dinary surge in the population of the country, a surge generated by an unprecedented increase in the number of births.

This swelling of the birth rate was to have two lasting effects on the nation. Obviously the increased population meant an increased consumer pool whose demand American industry expanded to meet. But, even more important, the age structure of the population altered substantially. The baby boom left a huge demographic bulge that, as it traveled through the age structure of the United States population, triggered sequential booms in baby food, bicycles, hula hoops, Coca-Cola, automobiles, and college enrollment. As the boom babies came of age, the bulge moved on into the housing market, with its effect first felt as a sharp rise in demand for apartments.

In order to fully understand how remarkable the phenomenon of the Apartment Boom was, it is necessary to recall that prior to the mid-'60s most owners of income property were pursuing a conservative investment course. In cities and towns around the country the neighborhood rooming house with its wide porches and shady trees was a symbol of solid stability. American writers from Mark Twain to Thomas Wolfe wrote about the owners of these rooming houses as sober, hardworking folk—the very opposite of the happy-go-lucky boomsters that had flocked to Chicago or Florida in search of quick riches. Though not all rental property could be defined as rooming houses, of course, the economic logic that governed all income properties was largely the same. Rental property was purchased to provide a steady, modest, and safe income for its owners. While the value of the property itself might rise somewhat with a maturing real estate market, such prices were of only secondary importance. The primary function of rental property was always to provide rents to the owners, so the value of the property depended on the amount of rental income it could produce.

In the mid-'60s however, boom babies were coming of age. As these young adults left home, demand for apartment housing soared. Builders responded quickly in major cities and college towns, but demand still outdistanced supply. Inevitably, this forced up rents, and as they rose, the reasons for investing in income property began to change subtly. Since the price of an apartment house had historically depended on the rental income it could produce for its owners, the jump in rent made

42

the property itself more valuable and its market value began to rise sharply. This jump in prices attracted attention and new buyers—people who had never before been interested in buying income property. As these new buyers entered the market, the apartment houses themselves began to acquire a scarcity value, and this was added to the selling price. Soon the prices of the apartment buildings were rising faster than the rents of the apartments themselves, and a fundamental tie that had restrained price rises in rental-income property for years was broken. Though the cost of rental housing was escalating far more rapidly than the rents owners could charge, investors didn't care. They were no longer pursuing a conservative investment course; they were buying into the rental property market in order to speculate on future price increases, and so the price of a piece of rental property began to float free of the actual income the property could ever be expected to produce.

With prices running far ahead of rental income, a negative cash flow was in effect for most investors; that is, the expenses required to own and maintain the property more than wiped out any rental income profits. Any profits would now depend on further appreciation of property values. This negative cash flow might have chilled the apartment boom had it not been for the passage of the Tax Reform Act of 1969. The new tax bill managed to reduce the tax advantages of other forms of investments and, in the process, made rental property even more attractive as an investment. Promoters were soon designing tax shelters that used the negative cash flow of income property to tax advantage. Employing high marketing fees, prepayment of interest, "wrap-around loans," "front-end points," and other exotic and often mysterious devices, promoters managed to give rental property a tax-shelter value that was often more precious to investors than the value of the property itself or the income it once produced. The negative cash flow that had resulted from the sharply increased prices actually increased the tax shelter value of rental property and made it even more attractive to investors.

By the end of 1969 the logic of real estate investment had begun to warp under the heat of the new money entering the market. For more than 20 years, real estate offices had seen young home buyers purchasing space within which to raise

43

their families, and people purchasing rental property as an investment in a safe and secure future. But this placid business climate soon began to feel the effects of the great gouts of cash that were gushing into the market. Real estate had become the fashion in investment. It was a hedge against a newly inflation-plagued economy. At cocktail parties and at bus stops, one could hear tales of enormous profits being won in the real estate market, while others told of dismal losses in the sagging stock market.

Faced with a bull market in rental real estate and a bear market on Wall Street, America's financial institutions began to figure on ways to help both. The solution was a money machine known as a Real Estate Investment Trust (REIT). REITs were devised to capitalize on a sharp divergence in interest rates that allowed the industry to borrow money continuously at low short-term interest rates while using the money for long-term construction and mortgage loans. The resulting income guaranteed large profits to the trusts and ever-increasing sums of money to feed the happily swirling financial vortex. Between 1969 and 1973, the asset base of the investment trusts increased from $2 billion to $20 billion, while the mortgage loans offered by commercial banks also skyrocketed from $66.7 billion in 1969 to $113.6 billion in 1973. With the difference in interest rates between short-term and long-term loans adding millions to the balance sheets of banks and mortgage companies, traditional caution and historical standards were abandoned and money flowed out like a swollen river.

Fueled by this floodtide of cash, speculation became rampant, based on the traditional boom assumption that prices could not help but continue to rise. With demand for rental housing still running strong, with plenty of investment capital available and with prices escalating weekly, there was a tremendous incentive to build new apartments. In a happy cycle, Wall Street promoted its lucrative REITs, providing money for investment to developers and builders who, in turn, sold to buyers who expected even greater price increases as their negative cash flow liability turned into a tax shelter benefit. The satisfied bankers saw what appeared to be a self-fueling money machine that purred merrily while spewing out rosy profits. Concrete trucks growled down California streets, their rotating drums flashing

44

the message: "Find a Need and Fill It." Construction dust layered the windows and desk tops in college towns. In Atlanta, a 14-month period saw the number of condominium starts jump from 14 to 187.*

Unfortunately, while the money machine hummed along and profits continued to file into their places on the balance sheets, the demographic bulge was moving on. Though the boom had seemed to be fueling itself in a cycle of self-fulfilling growth prophecy, a prophecy that seemed to have little to do with mere renters, suddenly the vacancies that were appearing in apartment houses and complexes around the country led many investors to wonder how an apartment building could continue to escalate in price when it was empty. The boom babies had grown older and they were entering the single family home market—a move prompted in no small measure by the high rents they had been forced to pay for their apartments. Across the country developers watched as the buildings that they had built, in the confident hope that they would be profit generators, stood empty and useless. The clear fact was that the market was oversupplied and, with sickening speed, investors realized it.

With catastrophic swiftness, the money machine sputtered to a stop. The financial superstructure collapsed, the REIT industry faced bankruptcy. A sudden upheaval in the nation's capital markets aggravated the severity of the crash. Faced with runaway, double-digit inflation, the government reduced the flow of money into the economy. Immediately, the prime rate rose to a prohibitive 12 percent. Mortgage rates climbed above 10 percent. The easy money that had financed the REIT industry, the builders, and the developers evaporated.

The REIT stocks dropped precipitously: Bank America Realty Investors, the Bank of America's REIT, fell from 32 in 1972 to a low of 6 in 1974; Wells Fargo Mortgage dropped from 26 to 2; Citizens and Southern Realty from 37 to 2; North American Mortgage Investors from 35 to 6; and Chase Manhattan Mortgage and Realty Trust plummeted from 70 to 4. The stocks of the builders and developers also plunged: U.S. Home from 37 to 2; and Kaufman and Broad from 52 to a low of 2. Many of

---

* *House and Home*, December 1976, p. 60.

the REITs and builders went bankrupt and their stocks no longer trade. The disaster that befell the real estate stocks during 1973 and 1974 was as great as the crash of 1929.

Prices of rental property collapsed to fifty cents on the dollar as bankrupt developers were forced to sell their property at auction. Apartment units begun dropped from their peak of 1,047,500 in 1972 to 268,300 in 1975. As foreclosures soared, banks across the country discovered how easily real estate loans suddenly became just plain real estate. By the end of 1976, 19 of the nation's largest banks held $1.2 billion worth of real estate taken through foreclosures, and $9.1 billion of their remaining $21.5 billion in real estate loans (42 percent) was either earning no interest whatsoever or the rates were reduced. In 1977 these institutions expected another $750 million to $1 billion in losses. Although most of these banks are in New York and Chicago, their unbidden properties are dispersed across the country and range from garden apartments to industrial parks.

Most of these properties came from troubled REITs. In order to avoid a total loss on their loans, banks had to take over the real estate in exchange for a reduction or cancellation of loans. Forcing the REITs into bankruptcy by simply calling the loans might have resulted in a complete loss. Many banks even accepted partially completed projects despite the expense of finishing them and the exposure of lawsuits from creditors.

Atlanta led the boom and was first to hit the skids. Along with the vacancy-plagued Coloney Square Complex and the $80 million Omni megastructure, there were still scores of unsold apartment buildings on the auction blocks, and some 30,000 vacant lots that will not be developed for a long time surround the city.

The National Bank of Georgia finally had to cut its dividend in August 1977 as a result of loan losses. Atlanta's largest bank, Citizens and Southern, followed in January 1978 for the same reason, the first time it had cut its dividend since 1906.

By mid-1978 Morgan Guaranty Trust Co. of New York, the leading lender on the Omni Project, finally announced it would foreclose, contending the project's owners and developers still owed nearly $77 million in principal and $14 million in interest.

Though perhaps Atlanta was hit hardest by the crash, the

rest of the country was not immune. By 1977, apartment owners and builders in Columbus, Ohio, were just beginning to recover from the collapse. At the same time, projections in Kansas City were that it would still be another two years before the new rental market would open up. In 1974 Union Bank of California had become the unwilling owner of an Orangetown, New York, complex, and as of August 1977 only 20 percent of it had been leased. Morgan Guaranty became the uneasy landlord of the exclusive Galleria complex on Manhattan's Upper East Side in October 1976. By August 1977 only 101 of the 253 condominiums had been sold.

Other banks across the country, including Citibank of New York, Chemical Bank, the Bank of America, Chase Manhattan Corp, and Bankers Trust Co. freely admit they are eager to get out of the real estate business. They were left holding the bag in the aftermath of the Apartment Boom.

The collapse of the Apartment Boom was every bit as dramatic as the crashes that had preceded it. In fact, more money may have been lost in the Apartment Crash than in any of the more celebrated crashes. But it remains an unheralded financial crisis, and the losses were absorbed largely by banks and other diversified institutions. Only those individuals who held stock in REITs or who could afford to play with tax shelter schemes were directly affected.

But perhaps the public's escape from the calamity of the Apartment Crash was not so fortunate as it would first appear. For the profit seekers and financial schemers did not leave the real estate market entirely. They simply followed the one-time boom babies into the single family home market. There the same ominous pattern of boom psychology is at work, and a crash this time will affect many, if not most, of us.

Part Two

Analysis

6

The Anatomy of a Boom

With a haunting generational regularity, the booms and crashes have come—as if these economic convulsions were a hereditary curse. From their lofty skyscraper vantage points, owners of the bankrupt REITs of the early '70s may have tried to look back across the years to the sad despair of their Chicago predecessors of more than a century ago. They certainly shared the same question as they surveyed their economic ruin—the question, "Why?" Why did the prices go up? Why did they peak? Why did things collapse just when everything looked so good? At regular 40- to 50-year intervals the great crashes have baffled generation after generation as they were swept to ruin. To each of them it must have seemed that an evil force had waited until the greatest number of optimistic people had climbed aboard the bandwagon before sending it careening over a cliff.

What causes the turn? This question invariably draws a simple smile and an answer armed with impregnable hindsight: "Prices got too high." The answer is, of course, correct. Yet every boom has found this hindsight as a residue of the boom that preceeded it, and in each boom time it has been ignored; for, after all, the most urgent question is, "How high is too high?" Sadly, this question has not brought a simple response because such an answer lies buried within the complex mathematical and emotional equations that make up the market. Thus, our examination of the anatomy of a boom must begin with the physiology of the marketplace.

The real estate market is hidden behind the fluttering flags at subdivision gates and the colorful signs that brokers put on the front lawn. To examine it, we will need to start with a more visible and easily measured market, the stock market.

The stock market is typical of all markets. Its liquidity, convenience, and visibility make its trends seem more dramatic, but the stock market is influenced by the same forces that affect all markets, including today's real estate market: fear, greed, and most important, anticipation. To illustrate the interaction of these primal forces on the market we will tell a true story that happened to one of the authors.

It was early January 1974. Gray was busy working in his office on a cold, wet afternoon when his stockbroker phoned. After the usual exchange of pleasantries, the broker came to the point.

"Ford Motor Company is selling at 40, one point from its low for the year and you should buy 500 shares on margin" (meaning that Gray would only have to put up half of the money, while borrowing the other half from the brokerage house). Gray was dumbfounded by the suggestion; just three months earlier the economy had been stricken by the Arab oil embargo. The market had dropped more than 200 points. We were all spending significant slices of our weekends idling in gas lines. Gray thought his broker had simply lost his mind. He was not sure that anyone would ever make another automobile. Who is going to buy stock in Ford Motors when they can't even buy gas? Gray diplomatically suggested to his broker that they would be better off in blimps.

But the broker did not give up easily. "The oil embargo is history," he countered, "and all these negatives you point out are already reflected in the price of the stock. People buy stocks for the future, not the past."

Though not by any means convinced, Gray finally struck a compromise with his crazy broker, bought 200 shares on a cash basis, and spent the rest of the afternoon with a critical case of buyer's remorse. For weeks, he was too embarrassed to tell anyone about his stupid purchase.

It was the middle of February when Gray noticed that Ford had somehow managed to struggle up five points. He had made $1,000 and was pleasantly baffled. Not wishing to look a gift horse in the mouth, he swiftly called his broker. Profit-taking seemed to him to be in order. But his broker was adamant. "I've seen these things before. Wait until the news turns good, then I'll tell you when to sell."

Gray didn't sell, but he did start paying a whole lot more attention to the market. He renewed his subscription to the *Wall Street Journal* and each morning he feverishly scanned the stock prices. It was as if Ford's quotation was printed in red letters and was the only quote on the page—he could find it that quickly. As the weeks passed Ford bobbed up and down, keeping the suspense building. By the fourth of March it had worked its way up to $47\frac{1}{8}$. Gray had now made $1,425. That afternoon, rumors that sounded solid were circulating, predicting that the OPEC nations were about to lift the boycott. Responding to the rumors, Ford jumped one and a quarter points the next day, closing at $48\frac{3}{8}$, only to be topped by a full two-point gain on March 6. Gray was now more than $2,000 richer and was finally beginning to get excited about Ford's prospects. If the oil embargo was really over, he reasoned, the gas shortage would soon be over and life could return to normal. Ford could resume making cars. He quickly bought 300 more shares at 50, and began to boast of his perceptive invest-

53

ment. Monday's close found Ford at 51½, and by week's end the embargo had been lifted. Within hours, Gray's stockbroker had his delighted client on the line. "It's time to sell," he said. Gray was incredulous. Calmly he asked if his broker had heard that the boycott had been lifted. The answer was, of course, yes, and the broker argued strongly against holding Ford any longer. Finally Gray agreed to sell the original 200 shares, but he insisted on holding on to the 300 shares he had purchased at 50.

It was a bad decision. The day in 1974 when the onerous embargo was lifted, the stock market peaked for the year. Ford reached 54 and then began to slip quickly. By midsummer the slippage became precipitous, and by October it had fallen below 30. By holding on to his 300 shares, Gray had not only wiped out all of the $2,400 profit he had made, but ended up $3,600 in the hole. But in Gray's folly there is a lesson to be learned.

All substantial markets are made up of hundreds of thousands of people, all as greedy as Gray was, and as if the market were a voting system, these people cast their thoughts with their money. The aggregate vote is amazingly accurate, but investors' thoughts are about the future. They anticipate the future with every purchase. An appraisal of Gray's experience with Ford shows how important this anticipation can be.

In the dark days of January 1974, with gas lines winding around the block and thermostats turned down to conserve fuel oil, the reality of the energy crisis was dawning on many Americans for the first time. It came as a shock. Since World War II we had never known energy conservation, nor had we ever questioned our abundant use of petroleum. When the ramifications of the oil shortage filtered down to average Americans, we were dazed. But while we were wondering about what had happened, the stock market (and Ford stock) had already anticipated the crisis. Prices fell. Then the direction of the anticipation turned. People began to buy on the assumption that things were likely to get better because they could hardly get worse. Analysts, looking at the economies of the OPEC nations, decided that the embargo could not last forever, for it would not benefit either the United States or the Arabs. So, looking ahead to the day when the embargo would be lifted, wise investors began to buy Ford. Under the pressure of their purchases, its price began to rise.

When the embargo was lifted, Ford stopped going up. The price had already risen to a substantial level on anticipation alone. Now the event that the investors had so confidently predicted had occurred. The price increase in Ford's stock had granted them large profits and it was time to move on to other things. Thus, Ford began to decline right in the face of the optimistic news.

This phenomenon of stock going up when the news is bad and down when the news is good makes no sense to many investors, who attribute it to a conspiratorial "they" who really control the market. However, Gray's experience with Ford shows us that the seemingly irrational downturns taken by the market in the face of optimistic news can be explained by an understanding of anticipation.

To be sure, Gray's experience with Ford was much simpler than the booms we have been examining, most of which lasted for much longer periods of time, and none of which revolved around as discreet an event as the Arab oil boycott. Still, anticipation remains the crucial factor in all of these economic collapses. To see why, we will need to expand the scope of our analysis.

In our Ford example, investors were anticipating a specific event—the lifting of the Arab oil embargo. In longer-term booms like our current housing boom, investors are anticipating not a specific event but the future occurrence of growth itself. This anticipation of growth can be termed a "growth assumption"; an assumption that a rate of growth established in the past will continue into the future. Once a growth assumption is widely held by investors, it begins to affect prices positively. In a situation where a growth assumption is at work, investors will buy because they anticipate future price increases. The effect of this anticipation on prices is known as a premium. Specifically, a *premium* is defined as the increase in price that is caused by a growth assumption.

Suppose, for example, we have some money to invest and we are hoping to get an 8 percent return on our investment. This return will either come in the form of immediate income, as an increase in the value of the thing we purchase over the length of time we own it, or as a combination of both. If we do not expect our investment to increase in value over the time we own it, our 8 percent will have to come from the immediate income our investment is producing. On the other hand, if the value of our holding is increasing at 8 percent each year, we will not need to receive any income from it at all. As you can see, our estimate of potential growth will be a very big factor in our determination of how much we will be willing to pay for the property; and indeed, in the market at large we can see that even a modest growth assumption will produce a premium and will raise the price significantly.

Imagine for a moment that we have a chance to buy a small hot dog stand. The hot dog stand is in a good location on a busy street corner and has posted a reliable yearly profit of $8,000 to its owners for some time. If we determine that there will be no increase in the value of the property given the current state of the hot dog stand market, we will pay no more than $100,000 because the income of $8,000 would represent the whole of our 8 percent return. Paying more than $100,000, we would earn less than our desired return. If, on the other hand, we happen to know that there is a strong market in hot dog stands, and that hot dog stand values have been growing at 3 percent annually for many years, the price situation changes. We will look carefully at the hot dog picture nationally and locally and might determine that our hot dog stand will, in all probability, be worth at least 3 percent more next year. Assuming this 3 percent growth in the value of the hot dog stand, we can pay up to $160,000 because, though the $8,000 we will receive in actual income from the hot dog sales will now be only 5 percent of the $160,000 sale price, when we add the 3 percent we expect in growth, we will come up with our desired 8 percent return. But look at how much more we will be paying to get into the hot dog business. With only a 3 percent growth assumption, the sale price has jumped a full $60,000! That $60,000 is the actual premium we, the buyer, will pay because of a 3 percent growth assumption that is attached to the hot dog stand. Note that this is an increase of a full 60 percent of the sale price. Think for a moment of the effect on prices if the growth assumption were 7 percent!

Growth Assumptions and Premiums

	0.0% GA*	3% GA	5% GA	6% GA	7% GA
Current return required under growth assumptions for an 8% total for return	8%	5%	3%	2%	1%
Premium in price	0.0	60%	166%	300%	700%
Dollar increase in price of the hot dog stand	0.0	$60,000	$166,000	$300,000	$700,000

* GA = growth assumption.

As you can see, in a time of rapidly increasing prices, it is growth assumptions that are putting steady pressure on the accelerator. Our chart seems to reduce the complexity of the market to algebraic simplicity, and indeed it *would* be just that simple if we had a crystal ball and could be certain of the accuracy of our growth assumption. Unfortunately we, like others, are forced to operate without the benefit of such a handy investment aid. Without sure knowledge of the future, a growth assumption is merely that: an assumption. An assumption that can be, and frequently is, wrong.

In our hot dog stand illustration, the assumption that the business will grow has caused a premium. If our assumption is correct, in a year we will be able to sell and make our 3 percent profit, *providing* we can find a buyer who will assume a 3 percent growth for yet another year. In order to make our projected 3 percent in price growth, we will raise the price of the hot dog stand to $164,800. Since the profits will have increased 3 percent to $8,240, our buyer will be making a 5 percent return on actual income. In order to make 8 percent, our buyer will have to assume that the growth rate will stay at 3 percent or more. If the buyer does assume this 3 percent growth, we will have a sale and all will be well.

But what if, when we are ready to sell, we cannot find a buyer that believes that the hot dog stand will grow in value at all? The business is exactly the same as when we bought it.

It still churns out hot dogs and is still earning a reliable $8,000 a year in profits. It seems reasonable that as there was no change in its income-producing ability, we should be able to sell it for the price we paid for it. But unfortunately, with no growth assumption, our business will sell for only $100,000 (the price a buyer can pay and make an 8 percent income from the $8,000 the stand produces), and we will have lost the $60,000 premium we paid assuming 3 percent growth. Thus, the existence of a premium can present a dangerous situation. If the growth outlook should look smaller, the premium will contract and prices will be lower.

Our experience with the hot dog stand has shown us the extent to which prices can be affected by growth assumptions, but does this explain the quantum acceleration in prices we have seen in the booms we've studied? At first glance we would have to answer no. The 3 percent growth rate we saw within the hot dog stand industry is certainly not a boom of the sort we are seeing in our current real estate market. Our hot dog stand had been expanding at the rate of 3 percent for many years, and we arrived at our growth assumption on the basis of careful research into the performance of that hot dog stand and other stands like it over a long period of time. In short, we were not speculating in any way. We were simply making what looked like a solid investment.

Still, if we look closely, we *can* see similarities between our investment experience and the classic booms of the past. We can see, for instance, that once growth is assumed, premiums expand and prices rise. We can see that this price rise will fuel even more optimistic growth assumptions which will expand premiums and prices still further. We can see, in other words, the rudimentary price spiral that in the boom times has become cyclonic—only a difference of degree. Let's pause for a moment to visualize this interaction of increasing growth assumption, expanding premiums, and accelerating prices.

Imagine that you are about to witness the first test flight of a newly designed missile. Your job is to estimate the highest elevation the missile will reach after it runs out of fuel. You are pitted against an opponent who will be doing the same thing. For weeks you have both been painstakingly preparing facts and figures to help you determine the performance limits of the

58

missile. The one whose estimate is the closest to the highest elevation reached by the missile after it runs out of fuel will win $10,000. During the flight you are free to raise and lower your estimates as long as the missile contains fuel. The missile should simply climb straight up until it runs out of fuel and then begin to fall back to earth. What is unknown to either of you is that inside the missile there is an electronic monitoring device. This device will monitor your estimates and will in turn control the missile's thrust. As you raise your estimates, the missile's thrust will increase. As you lower your estimates, the missile's thrust will decrease.

The missile blasts off from the launch pad. When it reaches a constant velocity the competition begins. Since this is the first test flight you and your opponent both file conservative estimates. As the missile ascends flawlessly you both gain confidence in its new design and file somewhat higher estimates. The higher estimates cause the missile's thrust to increase, increasing its velocity. Each second now the missile is picking up speed—it is accelerating. You observe the missile is now not only going higher, but it is also going higher faster. The fact that the missile is accelerating becomes the dominant factor—you both raise your estimates. Now the missile's speed increases even more each second—the added thrust increases acceleration. You both feverishly file higher and higher elevation estimates that cause the missile to leap ahead. The missile has now climbed much higher than you originally thought possible and is continuing to go faster and faster.

Suddenly your opponent lowers his estimate slightly. You pause. The information you had gathered over the past weeks in preparation is now apparently useless. This new design of missile is quite different from the ones you had studied. It has already surpassed your original expectations and right now it is still climbing faster each second. You wonder again why your opponent lowered his estimate. Then you remember—there is a limited amount of fuel on board the missile. You immediately file an estimate just below your opponent's. As you both begin to lower your estimates from their lofty levels, the missile's thrust begins to decrease. It is still accelerating—climbing at a faster rate each second—but it is accelerating at a lower rate than previously. Soon it becomes noticeable to both of you that the missile is not increasing speed as rapidly as before. This observation causes you to lower your estimates more significantly, which decreases thrust even more. Now the speed is no longer increasing—velocity is constant again. However, since your estimates are still higher than the missile's current altitude, you both lower them more. Now the thrust is even less and the missile is slowing down—velocity is decreasing. It appears now that the missile is running out of fuel. You both lower your estimates to very close to the missile's current elevation. The missile stops going up and begins to slip slowly backward toward earth.

But the missile still has fuel—the competition continues. Now you both lower your estimates a little below the current elevation. As you do, the thrust becomes less and the missile starts moving faster and faster downward—actually accelerating due to gravity. Now you are both feverishly lowering your estimates further and further below the elevation of the missile. The missile ultimately runs out of fuel and the competition ends.

The missile flight we have just described behaves like a boom, with the elevation of the missile corresponding to the level of prices. Just as your increasing confidence during the flight of the missile caused its rate of climb to increase, so investor confidence causes prices to rise, allowing investor confidence to increase still further. This is because confidence has spawned assumptions of further growth, and as we saw in the example of the hot dog stand, growth assumptions increase prices dramatically. As prices increase at faster and faster rates, growth assumptions increase in turn. This is the price spiral that is the heart of the boom

However, just as there was a point in the missile flight when the fact of limited fuel entered the consciousness of the contestants, there is a point in the flight of a boom when some participants will begin to wonder if the peak is not near. Their caution will cause growth assumptions to contract, even if only slightly. As we have seen, even a small reduction in a growth assumption will have a perceptible effect on prices, just as a slightly lower altitude estimate had a perceptible effect on the speed of the missile. Seeing the slower rate of price advance, other investors will respond with more cautious optimism, affecting prices still further. These subtle early alterations in price will probably not be noticed by the bulk of investors. But a reverse spiral has begun. As the number of investors registering conservative growth estimates increases, prices will continue to respond until doubt is widespread and growth assumptions turn flat. Prices will respond by rising less rapidly, leveling, and ultimately falling. As the decline becomes apparent the downward spiral will be reinforced by even more panicky investors until, like our missile, prices are plunging.

The flight of the missile demonstrates the crucial effect of growth assumptions and resultant premiums on the flight of a boom. Near the peak of a boom, prices, premiums, and growth assumptions are all accelerating upward. In the depths of a crash they are all accelerating downward.

This is the price spiral at work in our current boom. Currently it is going up, but for how much longer? Let's look.

Part Three

Real Estate Today

7

The Housing Boom
of the 1970s

We are now in the midst of what may be the greatest and most destructive boom of them all: the Housing Boom of the 1970s. Following patterns we have seen so many times before, investors in cities and towns across the nation are looking at single family homes as a secure path to fortune.

Just as every boom we have examined in this book began with investments that were prudent and sound, today's housing boom was once based on a happy intersection of four very fortunate conditions in the early '70s. The children of the baby boom were coming out of college and into the prime home-buying ages of 25 to 34. The arrival of this huge generation meant a bulging demand for homes. This demand, which was coupled with the continuing suburban migration and the regulations and restrictions generated by a new environmental consciousness, led to a shortage of land. With the price of land rising, along with inflated costs for labor and materials, new homes began to cost more. Yet this same inflation only burnished real estate's popularity as an inflation hedge. Moreover, the attractiveness of real estate was almost guaranteed by federal tax codes that continued to give it preferential treatment.

These fortunate conditions—the increased housing demand spawned by the postwar baby boom, the scarcity value that had been attached to the price of land, the value of real estate as an inflation hedge, and tax advantages—assured that real estate would be the best investment for many years to come.

As the Vietnam War ended, the Housing Boom, fueled by these optimistic conditions sputtered into life. At the end of 1971 the median price of a newly completed single family home was a quite modest $25,300. In 1972, the year the market first began to heat up, this price increased $4,400 to $29,700 by year end. Beginning in 1973 the pace of economic events began to pick up. During the year several commodity shortages developed, including a shortage of lumber. As the prices of lumber pushed higher, so did the cost of homes. The effect of this lumber shortage on the home-building industry was aggravated still further in 1974 as the increased price of oil was reflected in the prices of construction materials ranging from tarpaper and shingles to linoleum. The inflationary effects of these and many other shortages inspired price increases and prompted caution in the nation's money markets. But, though prices were

66

higher and money was tight, real estate was seen as an inflation hedge and demand did not slacken. By the end of 1973 the median price of a new home climbed $6,000 to $35,700, and even with a tight mortgage market, the price of a new home in 1974 struggled upward a surprising $1,700 to $37,400.

By the end of 1975 the new home that would have sold for $25,300 four years earlier was being purchased for $42,100, a $4,700 gain for the year. Of course, folks who had purchased their homes prior to 1972 were finding that their total assets had increased considerably. More and more often one would hear discussions of real estate over lunch or in hotel lobbies. The single family housing market was showing remarkable persistence in the face of a shaky economy. Though daunted slightly by setbacks in the economy as a whole, prices were still advancing by respectable percentages year after year. If the virtual shut-down of the mortgage market in 1974 could not cool the market, what could? Thus investors reasoned.

In 1974 and 1975 America was in a postwar recession. Trying to prod a speedy recovery, the Federal Reserve system allowed a much freer flow of money into the economy. The effect of this on the single family home market was to become dramatic. Real estate values, which had managed to grow even without the nourishment of easy credit, began to expand when more money became available.

In 1975 the volume of mortgage loans offered by savings and loan associations climbed to a record $88 billion. Many of these loans were offered to people for whom traditional lending standards had been considerably relaxed. Prior to the mid-'70s most savings and loans would not, as a matter of policy, grant a mortgage on a house that cost more than twice the buyer's gross yearly income. By 1975, however, with housing prices accelerating much more rapidly than wages, and with demand for loans at record highs, lending institutions relaxed these standards, often granting mortgages for property that was valued at three times the buyer's income.

Meanwhile, the economy at large was in the grip of an economic anomaly called "stagflation"—stagnation while the inflation rate was still increasing. This meant a slack demand for corporate loans. Banks across the country compensated by putting even more of their idle funds into mortgages, and by 1976

67

all memory of the once-tight mortgage market was forgotten. In 1976 the median cost of a new home jumped $3,800 to $45,900.

By the middle of 1976, as the economic pace quickened, it was evident that the house-building industry around the country was running at full throttle. In September of 1976, Dallas, Texas, reported single family housing construction starts had increased by a third. In Fort Worth the jump in new housing construction was more than 40 percent over the year before. By the end of 1976 most contractors in Denver, Colorado, were no longer accepting new orders because they were working on backlogs that stretched as far as six months. A large building contractor with offices in Colorado, Arizona, New Mexico, and Texas recorded a 25 percent jump in sales during 1976, while estimating that the newly finished homes had increased in value by more than 12 percent for the year. A national magazine quoted a developer in Clearwater, Florida, as saying that his area "was in a full boom situation," with single family home sales doubling in two years.*

By 1977, the real estate industry was indeed in a full-boom situation. The median price of a new home had more than doubled since the beginning of 1972.

The money lending industry began to design mortgage schemes to make loans even more attractive. One such scheme was the gradual-payment mortgage, which allowed small initial payments, with larger payments deferred until later in the mortgage period when, it was assumed, inflation and career development would make the larger payments more affordable. Generally, the full payment level would not be reached for five years.

The Bank of America (the world's largest bank) and Home Savings and Loan (the largest savings and loan) introduced an investment that revolutionized the mortgage-financing industry. It was called the Mortgage Passthrough. These passthroughs were sold to individual investors whose capital was lent out as single family mortgages. In effect, investors bought first mortgages. The promotion of public investment in single family mortgages was a natural response to the growing de-

* *House and Home,* December 1976.

68

mand for financing. The success of the passthrough made the mortgage market available to Wall Street's enormous bond market. It, like the REITs during the Apartment Boom, provided an almost endless source of risk capital to finance the boom in single family houses. Through these new mortgage schemes the money pool that was tapped by home buyers increased sharply.

The torrents of money pouring forth from lending institutions were not to go to waste in 1977, for a virtual buying frenzy was on. A major source of this frenzied demand for homes proved to be first-time home buyers. As the word of the relentless rise of real estate prices spread, there was a growing sense of panic among those who had not yet entered the home-buying market. With the prices of homes far outdistancing any increases in wages or inflation, many young would-be home-owners decided that it was now or never for them. There was a growing perception that prices were as low as they were ever going to be. "A lot of the buying in this country is panic buying," the *Wall Street Journal* observed, "People are buying now because they think they'll never have another chance."

This panic-buying reaction indicated that no one perceived the prices of homes as unrealistically high. As in similar past situations, many people who have jumped into today's housing boom have not seen it as a boom. They have simply seen it as the way the future will look.

The *Journal* also summed up the national situation in 1977:

> From Southern California, where lotteries often determine who gets to order a new house, all the way to New Jersey, where some developers this year have already exceeded sales for all of 1976, demand is far outstripping builders' capacity to deliver new houses.
>
> Instead of a firm sales contract, more and more prospective buyers in places like Denver, Houston and Washington D.C., are being offered only a spot on the waiting list.*

With phenomenal price increases, the housing market was attracting more speculators, who bought homes strictly for the prospect of future price increases. In some states this specula-

* *Wall Street Journal*, May 24, 1977.

tive buying was so widespread that severe housing shortages began to develop. One California builder was forced to put up signs on sale properties that read, "Our homes are planned for owner occupants and not for investor/speculators."* Another large corporation put signs in the windows of its offices with the slogan, "We sell to the needy not the greedy."†

Speculative activity was not confined to newly built homes. The median price of existing homes had been increasing at a steady rate in the five years 1972 through 1976, finishing the year in 1976 at $39,000.‡ But in 1977 the rate of increase leaped ahead. In May 1977 the price had increased $3,200, and by July existing homes were selling for $43,700, a $4,700 increase in six months that added up to an annual growth rate of more than 20 percent. These price increases helped to fuel the boom as homeowners traded up, using their increased equity to finance new down payments for their new home investments.

Terrance and Sherilyn Odo are examples of this investment strategy. Terrance and Sherilyn are both airline employees in their early thirties. They have two children and bring home an annual combined income of $24,000. The Odos were living in a condominium they had purchased three years before. After watching the value of their condominum increase over several years, the Odos sold it for a profit of $18,000 which they used to finance a $71,000 three-bedroom home. Just six months after the purchase of this home the Odos were confident they could sell it for $110,000. "It's just a pleasant house that no one would go screaming after," Mrs. Odo told a reporter. "We don't have a lot of money . . . there's no way we could save $40,000, and yet we've made that much in six months on our house." Because of this windfall, the Odos took turns standing in line for two nights and a day in order to sign up for a new $111,500 four-bedroom house. To purchase it and to keep their monthly payments at a bearable $630 a month, the Odos planned to put $60,000 down.§ The down payment alone was more than twice their annual income. They had the money because they shrewdly played a boom market.

* *San Francisco Examiner and Chronicle*, May 1, 1977.
† *New West*, June 6, 1977.
‡ National Association of Realtors.
§ *Wall Street Journal*, May 24, 1977.

As more and more speculators bought houses for the expected price rise, competition increased to find renters that would help offset the burden of monthly payments and maintenance costs. By June 1977 homes for rent in the San Francisco area actually outnumbered houses for sale. Normally, homes for sale outnumber rentals by more than ten to one.*

Pressured by panic buying and speculation, prices in some areas of the country have accelerated at incredible rates. In Contra Costa County, just east of San Francisco, the selling price of the average home advanced at a 46 percent annual rate for the first four months of 1977.†

With 20 percent down this translated to 230 percent profit in one year! Using second mortgages, the speculator's common tool, only 10 percent down payment was required. That degree of leverage produced a 460 percent annual profit.

The nation's builders were profiting handsomely too. The average earnings of ten top builders in 1977 were more than twice their 1976 earnings.

As 1977 progressed a new area of the real estate market began to bubble and boil. That new area was condominiums. The word from Chicago and St. Louis was "condomania." In Chicago the prices of many condominiums tripled and even quadrupled in less than two years. Many buyers in choice areas doubled their money on resales in five months.

This trend was sweeping the country's major metropolitan areas, gobbling up 50 percent of the for-sale market in southern California, Chicago, Washington, D.C., southern Florida and San Francisco.

The situation was explosive—buyers were as anxious to buy as the sellers were to sell. The sellers had made huge quick profits and the buyers expected to do the same.

In Chicago, speculators even moved into rental buildings in anticipation of their conversion to condominiums, for renters in a building being converted to condominiums generally got first chance at the units and a 5 to 10 percent discount off the price to the public.

Banks were becoming big winners at condomania with profitable loans at 13 to 14 percent interest plus three points for the

* *Wall Street Journal*, June 2, 1977.
† Contra Costa Board of Realtors.

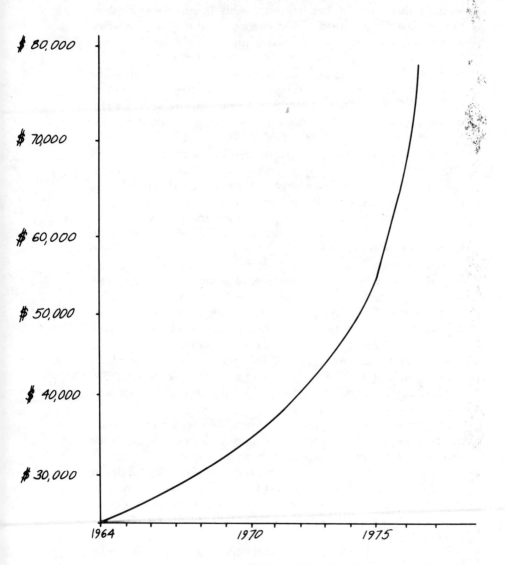

AVERAGE HOME PRICE
CONTRA COSTA COUNTY, CALIFORNIA

SOURCE: CONTRA COSTA BOARD OF REALTORS

loan, which can increase the annual rate to more than 20 percent depending on the length of the repayment period. Thus banks were often willing to finance 100 percent of the purchase price of a building.

Throughout 1977 and 1978 prices of single family homes and condominiums continued to rise rapidly. Speculative activity, which originally had been confined primarily to California and a few large metropolitan areas, began to break out in cities and towns all over the nation. Stockbrokers found clients selling out stocks almost weekly to buy real estate. Many borrowed against their stocks from their brokers to buy houses. *Fortune* commented on the unusually high margin debt in a nonspeculative market. The magazine concluded that a lot of real estate was being financed by Wall Street. Even teachers who had been saving for years in their tax-deferred retirement plans were cashing them to buy additional houses. The riches granted to those speculating in real estate seemed to dwarf the 8 percent, compounded, tax-free return available for teachers' retirement.

There seemed no escape from the barrage of fliers in the mail, ads on radio and television, alluring articles in the newspapers, and exotic business cards stuck in the cracks of front doors. Renters were constantly reminded of the thousands of dollars they were losing each year by not purchasing a home.

Even brokerage firms were promoting real estate investments and holding their own real estate seminars. Local newspapers carried real estate columns that resembled "Dear Abby."

Typical letters read like this one in the September 25, 1977, edition of the *Contra Costa Times*:

> Dear Mr. Hall:
> We own about a dozen single family rentals. Over the years we have accumulated these properties by refinancing some of the originals and buying others. This was possible because of the rapid increase in the value of the original rentals.
> Today we figure we have an equity of about $400,000. However, we are still working our tails off and don't receive one cent of spendable income. Is this what you call a good investment?

73

Throughout the rest of 1977 and 1978 people from every conceivable walk of life caught speculation fever. Supermarket checkers, firefighters, doctors, schoolteachers, all had set their sights on a fortune in real estate. Optimism ran high. The party seemed to be just beginning.

8

Understanding the Housing Boom

When early scientists were first beginning to study animal anatomy, they based their observations about the living upon data collected through examination of the dead. Through dissection they were able to identify and describe the functioning of an animal's heart, lungs, and muscles. From these findings they were able to discover the interrelationships that existed between these essential biological components—interrelationships that accounted for the vitality of the animal. Yet these observations and deductions had to happen when life was no longer present, when the systems no longer functioned.

In our analysis of the current Housing Boom, we are in much

the same position as these early physiologists. We have been dealing thus far with the booms and busts that have afflicted our economy in the past; economic episodes that are dead and accessible to our scalpel. But now we must begin our examination of our own living boom, where the anatomy we have uncovered is again obscured.

Take speculation, for example. In all of the booms we have studied in this book there have been feverish levels of speculation that have acted to push prices ever higher. Moreover, while any sober examination of today's real estate market will disclose the fact that ours is an equally speculative market, we are confident that most of the readers of this book who own property today do not think of themselves as speculators. All of us feel a certain smugness when we look at the booms and crashes we have described in this book, a certain sense that speculation is risky and irresponsible and that our boom-time predecessors received their just deserts. We, however, are not like them. We know that our intention is not speculative. We are simply buying a home.

It is clear that the reason so many of us refuse to see the current escalation of housing prices as a boom is related to our refusal to see ourselves as speculators. We, like millions of Americans, are unable or unwilling to see that the sober, responsible act of buying a home in today's feverish housing market could be called speculation. We are more than willing to describe ourselves as homeowners or investors, but we balk at the idea that we might be speculators. Since we recognize that investors in a highly speculative market are speculators by definition, we try to deny that the market is in fact speculative. We try to convince ourselves that the current price increases, meteoric as they are, are simply "the way it is." Thus, in our boom as in every other boom we have investigated, the extent of speculation is obscured.

Similarly, our anatomy of a boom disclosed the crucial importance of premiums to the progress of a rapidly expanding market. We have seen that premiums are like uranium in the reactor of a boom. They are the fuel that keeps prices rising until, inevitably, they get too high. But again, in our current boom home buyers don't seem worried that they might be paying excessive premiums—premiums that could evaporate with catastrophic financial results—because the prices they are paying for a house do not seem that much higher than the cost of the material and labor required to build it. How, they ask, can the price of a home fall below the amount of money required to build it? Since the prices paid for supplies, labor, and land appear to be going up each year, can't we expect that housing prices will at least keep abreast of these increases?

Unfortunately, as important as growth assumptions and premiums are to the anatomy of a boom, they are elusive and not easily detectable. Like cancer in the tissues of a living organism, premiums infect at many different levels within a healthy market. Without being clearly seen, premiums begin to affect prices throughout the market.

When growth is assumed in the price of a house, that price will contain a premium. And since all the materials that go into the house are purchased from markets that also respond to supply and demand, they will soon reflect a growth assumption (and a premium) of their own. As premiums expand, prices rise, new construction increases and so does demand for commodities from land to shingles. As the premium within the sale price of a house expands, so do premiums contained within the prices charged in subsidiary markets. The price of lumber, for example, contributes to the cost of a house, and the price of lumber fluctuates greatly, reflecting the demand for housing. So does the price of land. If the housing market is rapidly expanding and prices are rising for houses, these commodities will also show increases. They will begin to show premiums within their own prices. Thus, measuring the value of a house by means of its constituent costs is misleading. For should demand for houses decline, premiums will contract and prices will drop on all levels of the housing industry. It will simply cost less to build a house.

Although a drop in construction costs may seem like an unprecedented occurrence, it has happened many times in the past. From 1941 through 1944, construction costs dropped 12½ percent. From 1937 through 1939 costs fell 8½ percent. The largest drop recorded to date was from 1929 through 1934, when construction costs plunged 39 percent. Other notable periods of decline were 1891, 1895, 1897 through 1899, 1901, 1903 through 1904, 1911, 1921, and, more recently, 1960 through 1962

77

and 1970. Land costs also fluctuate, as can be seen from the tables on page 91. Thus building costs move up or down depending on the demand for the final product: houses. As the demand for and prices of houses decline, building and land costs decline accordingly. Commodities drop first and then labor costs abate as unions are forced by their constituents to shift emphasis from higher wages to more employment. The high profit margins awarded home builders for the past few years will evaporate as more new homes compete for fewer buyers, bringing building costs and selling prices closer.

When we began our research for this book, we wanted to find out why today's Housing Boom was not being widely perceived as a boom, why the dangers of a superheated market were not being widely discussed. In order to find answers for these questions we have talked to scores of investors. The answers we received disclose more than a lack of understanding of the nature of speculative activity and premiums and their effects on prices; the most striking lack of understanding was of history itself. In our boom, investors are putting their money into a highly speculative market hoping for a large return on their investment while at the same time denying any speculative intent. This denial is not unusual. It has been true of speculators in every major boom we've seen. In our boom, investors argue that prices are at their natural levels and that they will naturally go still higher. This argument completely ignores the volatile nature of premiums and growth assumptions, but such ignorance is not unusual either. It also has been true in each of our historical examples. There are many examples in the history of markets similar to our current housing market. But these examples are not widely known. They are not taught in our schools, they don't appear in our morning papers.

We have seen that the booms of history have seemed to come at fairly regular intervals. Our discussions with investors in today's real estate market indicate that they are as uninformed about the economic disasters that struck their predecessors as those predecessors were of those that preceded them. Thus we are forced to conclude that our anatomy of a boom would be incomplete without a recognition of the crucial importance of historical ignorance to the life of a boom.

Historical ignorance, of course, does not necessarily indicate thoughtlessness. On the contrary, today's real estate investors are usually very thoughtful people who have solid reasons for their optimism. Today's housing boom, as we have seen, was once based on the increased housing demand spawned by the postwar baby boom, the scarcity value that has been attached to the price of land, the value of real estate as a hedge against increasing inflation, and the advantages that the U.S. tax codes have given real estate investment. These conditions have lent support to real estate as a sound investment and have served to dazzle investors into a dreamy ignorance of the profound and dangerous changes that have taken place within the market. Make no mistake, the conditions listed above *have* been fortunate. They have all furnished sound reasons for investing in real estate, but they have also fueled a boom, a market phenomenon with a life and destiny of its own.

Upon close examination, it becomes easy to see how the four fundamental conditions of population, land, inflation, and taxes have served to blind investors to the reality of a boom market. They are all good reasons; perhaps, ironically, too good, for they have furnished the glossy hide that has prevented Americans from seeing the progressive spread of speculation and the expansion of premiums that are attacking the vital organs of the market. In their attempt to deny or ignore the speculative nature of today's real estate market, investors have turned these optimistic conditions into articles of faith, gambling that as long as they remain in effect prices will continue to rise. This belief, unfortunately, not only ignores the clear and present danger that is always inherent in a boom, it also ignores some basic changes that have taken place within the fundamental conditions themselves. As fortunate as population structure, land, inflation, and taxation have been for real estate, today none of these four conditions is as impregnably optimistic as it once appeared.

9

Population

Population has been perhaps the most celebrated reason for investing in real property. As we saw in our account of the Apartment Boom of the early part of this decade, the postwar spurt in the nation's birth rate sent a cresting wave of consumers rippling through the economy. Inevitably, they began to buy houses—in unprecedented numbers. This surge in demand has had an immediate and forceful effect on housing prices. It seems reasonable to assume that prices will reflect the demand represented by boom babies for some time to come. In fact, on the basis of current demographic data, many housing experts are projecting a continued high demand into the mid-1990s.

In analyzing past population projections and the actual patterns that subsequently unfolded, we have found that there are no experts when it comes to projecting future population trends.

During the depression days of the '30s, the birth rate was an extremely low 2½ million per year. The United States was viewed by the demographers of that time as a mature society, and they saw little likelihood of a meaningful jump in the number of children Americans would have. But suddenly in 1940 the birth rate began to expand and was to reach 3.8 million in 1947. The baby boom had dawned.

Enamored with this new high birth rate, Equitable Life Assurance Society, in the summer of 1963, built a huge pavilion for the New York World's Fair that housed a display they called a Demograph. The Demograph was a 45-foot electronic map of the United States with an umbilical line to the Census Bureau. It clicked off births state by state and recorded an up-to-the-minute total of the U.S. population in illuminated numbers six feet high. The Demograph was a celebration of the future by Equitable, whose experts predicted that the company's assets would rise from their then current $10.8 billion to $16 billion as the U.S. population increased to well over 210 million. These projections were, of course, based on the tremendous increase in the nation's birth rate since the war.*

Nine eventful years later, Equitable's assets had indeed reached 16.4 billion dollars, but the baby boom had, curiously enough, acted like any other boom. Just when Equitable and many others were planning on its increase, the birth rate declined sharply. The company's estimates turned out to be far too optimistic. Its guess was nearly two million people too high.

Since 1957, when the birth rate began its decline, a perplexed Census Bureau has repeatedly lowered its estimates and long-term forecasts. As the birth rate dropped, explanations changed and we began to read about the shift to smaller families, then about the trend of families postponing the first child, and finally articles about the impact of new birth control methods. With the birth rate below depression levels,† 1976 heard bleak predictions once again.

* *Barron's*, December 6, 1977.

† On a births-per-thousand basis we were far below the birth rate experienced in the 1930s.

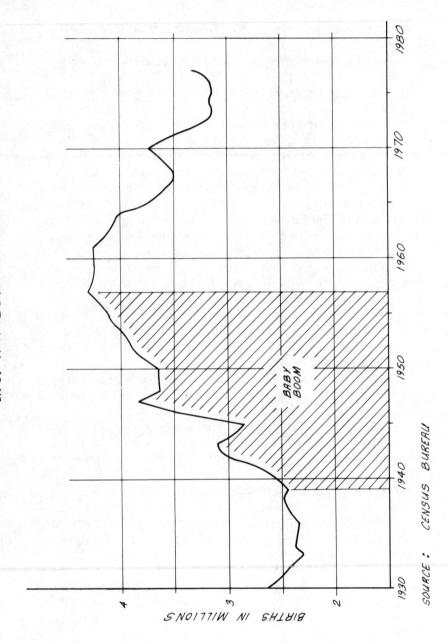

U.S. NUMBER OF BIRTHS

BABY BOOM

BIRTHS IN MILLIONS

4

3

2

1930   1940   1950   1960   1970   1980

SOURCE : CENSUS BUREAU

82

Initially, this baby bust seems odd when one looks at the age structure of the population. The couples that were not having babies were the offspring of the postwar boom. During the late '60s and early '70s, women were arriving at prime child-bearing age in record numbers. Why were they waiting? Looking closely at housing prices and birth rates, it seems likely that an average-income couple couldn't afford a house and children at the same time. This explanation seems even more likely when we consider the fact that in mid-1977 six out of ten couples buying their first home were using two incomes to do so.* With the future mother's income needed for mortgage payments there simply was not enough time and money for children.

In 1977 the nation's birth rate reversed and climbed 7 percent.† If our conjecture is accurate, this could indicate that most of the families now having children already have a house, which in turn could indicate that the demand furnished by first-time home buyers is diminishing.

But even if our conjecture is not accurate, there will still be an end to the increased demand represented by the postwar generation. People get older, and sooner or later the postwar baby bulge will pass through the home-buying ages. When it does a decrease in demand will occur. Since the birth rate declined rapidly after the baby boom of the late '40s and early '50s, there simply will be fewer people coming into home-buying ages in the near future than there are now.

The fact that demand will eventually drop is, of course, recognized by housing experts, but their estimates vary considerably as to when it will happen. In numerous economic forecasts, we are given estimates ranging from the mid-1980s to the mid-1990s.

Divining the time when this demographically determined drop in demand will occur would seem to be a straightforward calculation. Applying the axiom that most people buy houses between the ages of 25 and 34, we can simply examine the age structure of the population and should be able to come up with the year that demand will peak (as well as the rate of increase

* *Time*, September 12, 1977.
† *Barron's*, December 26, 1977.

before and the rate of decline after this peak). The problem with this calculation is that the axiom no longer holds true. It is no longer true that 25-to-34-year-olds are buying the majority of the houses. Savings and loan associations reported in 1976 that most home buying was being done by people from the ages of 30 to 44.* Projecting *these* ages out and including the boom-baby bulge in the figures, it is possible to predict a demand that will extend into the 1990s. But there is another complication. According to the Federal Home Loan Bank Board, 65 percent of the people buying homes in 1976 were trading up. These individuals were selling one house to buy another, which obviously does not add to overall demand for housing. When the postwar population bulge first entered the market, as first-time home buyers, it represented an enormous increase in overall demand. This increase in demand drove prices up and granted enormous increases in equity to older homeowners. These people often used the increased value of their property to finance a trade-up to larger and more expensive homes. But as the rate of first-time home buying declines, so will overall demand. This can have a profound effect on the market, for as demand slackens so will pressure on prices. If prices slow their rate of advance, older homeowners will no longer be able to finance their trade-ups. Thus the level of overall demand is crucial to our investigation of prices, and overall demand still rests totally on the demand represented by boom babies who are entering the housing market for the first time.

According to a study based on the 1970 census, 33 percent of all households in this country owned their own homes before the age of 25,† 55 percent from the ages of 25 to 29, 71 percent from the ages of 30 to 34, and 77 percent from the ages of 35 to 44. A close look at this study reveals that demand for houses declines as people get older. While 33 percent of Americans who were aged 20 to 24 owned their own homes, this figure increased to 55 percent for the age group of 25 to 29. Since 33 percent of the latter group already owned their homes before

* *Challenge*, November-December 1976.

† Because a significant number of those under 25 might still be living in the households of their parents, the 33 percent figure would be higher than the actual figure. This factor would become negligible in the 25–29 and older groups.

84

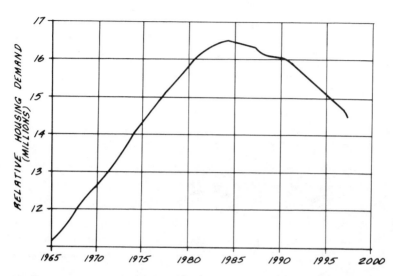

PROJECTED HOUSING DEMAND
BASED ON THE 1970 CENSUS

This graph shows the number of first-time home buyers based on the age structure of the U.S. population. Projections are based on the 1970 census. Demand will begin to level off in the early 1980s, peak in 1984, and decline thereafter.

they turned 25, only 22 percent of the 25 to 29 age group actually purchased homes for the first time. Similarly, only 16 percent of the 30-to-34 age group and only 6 percent of those aged 35 to 44 are first-time home buyers. As we move into the 45 and older group there is actually declining ownership, or net selling. By applying *these* figures to the age structure of the population and projecting the result we can predict that housing demand will peak in the early 1980s. The above graph illustrates this peak.

Still, even on the basis of these more conservative calculations, it seems reasonable for investors to remain optimistic at least for the short term since the peak in demand is expected no earlier than the first years of the next decade. The trouble with this reasoning is that it ignores the basic nature of the marketplace, which tells us that demand nearly always occurs

85

FAMILIES AFFORDING
A NEW HOUSE

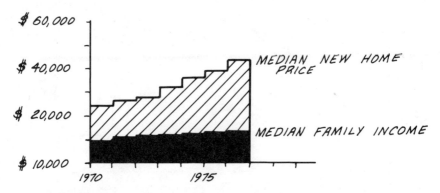

This graph shows that home prices have increased much faster than income levels. With this assumed to continue, houses are as cheap today as they ever will be.

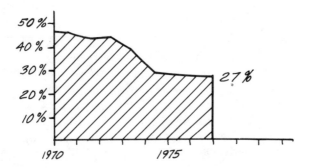

This graph illustrates the declining percentage of families that can afford a new home. In 1977 only 27% could afford a new home.

SOURCE: M.I.T HARVARD JOINT CENTER
FOR URBAN STUDIES

86

and peaks sooner than is expected. With the prices of houses increasing faster than the levels of income, buying a house as soon as possible has seemed a necessity to many Americans. The number of families that could actually afford the average house in 1977 was nearly half of what it was in 1970.*

Millions of Americans, believing that prices will continue to increase rapidly, have concluded that a house is as cheap today as it will ever be, that if they wait, the home they want will simply not be affordable any longer. Thus, millions of people are making tremendous sacrifices to buy houses they cannot afford.

Moreover, increasing prices have brought investment value and have made property even more attractive to those who can afford it. Due to feelings of urgency or greed, millions of Americans have been persuaded to buy homes immediately. This has had a profound effect on the structure of demand, and it suggests that demand will peak much sooner than straight demographic projections would suggest.

The facts of the previously cited boom in apartments during the early years of this decade furnish a concrete historical example of this phenomenon. The normal ages used in predicting demand for apartments range between 18 and 25. If we project these ages out from the baby boom in the same manner as many experts are now doing for housing demand, we find that the peak demand for apartments should have occurred sometime close to 1977. In fact, the peak occurred in 1972.

If this demand pattern holds true for single family homes, it means that the peak has already happened or will in the very near future. While it is impossible to predict the precise moment the peak will occur, it *is* possible to predict what will happen when it does. Just as the marketplace has for years anticipated increases in demand for housing, it will begin to anticipate the decline. The effect of this negative anticipation on prices is obvious—and ominous.

* Based on the definition of *afford* in the M.I.T.-Harvard study.

10

Land

As the changing structure of the nation's population has increased housing prices, land prices have also risen sharply. The tremendous increase in land prices over the last few years was a result of several factors that occurred at nearly the same time. Besides the arrival of boom babies at home-buying age, land prices were stimulated by the dramatic migration of urban and rural residents to suburban areas surrounding the large cities, and by a sharp increase in the level of foreign investment in U.S. land.

The rush of urbanites to the suburbs in recent years occurred for many of the same reasons a similar migration occurred during the 1920s when Florida and other outlying areas were "discovered." Not unlike the '20s and their Coolidge Prosperity, the 1960s were prosperous times for most Americans. In both eras, people appeared to yearn for escape from the cities that were responsible for their prosperity. By the early to mid-

'60s, American cities were suffering some severe problems. Pollution was becoming more and more of a problem; the crime rate in most urban areas was increasing to the point where people began to feel unsafe on the streets; racial tensions were increasing, and the quality of the public schools was declining. These and other reasons led many families to leave the city and settle into suburban communities where they were joined by people who were moving into large metropolitan areas from rapidly mechanizing rural America. The latter folk, moving nearer to the large industrial areas where the new jobs were located, often avoided the central cities for much the same reasons as their ex-urbanite neighbors. Federal and state governments facilitated this migration with huge road-construction projects that eventually linked the suburbs to the central city. Two-car garages became commonplace as we grew into a full-fledged automobilized society.

Added to the new suburbanites' demand for land was a sharp increase in the amount of foreign investment in U.S. land. This new demand developed in the mid-1970s, and was spawned by the fact that while inflation was bad in the United States, it was horrendous elsewhere. Foreign nationals, seeing U.S. land prices running ahead of inflation began to invest heavily. The extent of this foreign investment has been difficult to judge specifically, but in the San Francisco Bay Area, for example, investors from Iran, Saudi Arabia and Hong Kong were purchasing enough property to be seen by real estate observers as a significant force on local markets.

Though this combination of foreign investment, suburban migration, and an increasing pool of potential home buyers added up to a historically unprecedented level of demand, the amount of land available at the perimeters of metropolitan areas should have been adequate to absorb all of these new buyers; and indeed the land rush was absorbed until recent years. The statistics are interesting: in 1890, the cost of land accounted for nearly 40 percent of the total price of a single family home. By 1953, however, this figure had dropped to a mere 17 percent.* As these figures indicate, in the early years of the suburban land rush, land itself was quite cheap. In those years it was

* Historical Statistics of the U.S.—Colonial Times to 1957, pp. 388–89.

only necessary to buy a parcel of land and build houses on subdivided lots. When the development was finished, developers had to do little more than drive a half-mile farther and start over again.

Eventually, communities became appalled at this burgeoning suburban sprawl and began to incorporate and enact much stricter zoning codes than developers had ever encountered previously. Additionally, a growing environmental concern fostered a labyrinth of overlapping state and federal regulations. These restrictions and regulations not only increased the cost of developing land, they also extended the lead time required to develop land from months to years, which had the effect of limiting supply in the face of unparalleled demand. A recent Rutgers University survey of 2,000 builders concluded that "excessive" regulation of all kinds now accounts for $9,844, or almost 20 percent, of the cost of a new $50,000 house. Notice that this 20 percent is not the cost of regulation per se, but only regulations the study found to be excessive.

A representative example of the effect of public policy decisions on home prices is furnished by Fairfax County, Virginia, where officials responded to flourishing demand by halting all construction for the 18 months it took to draw up a master plan for development.* By the time this moratorium was lifted, demand had soared to levels that were impossible to accommodate, and prices skyrocketed. A banker in Morris County, New Jersey, meanwhile, claimed that as a result of recent environmental regulations, an $8,000 lot may cost as much as $8,000 more before construction can proceed.† His is a frequently heard complaint.

This combination of mushrooming demand and shrinking supply has resulted in a sharp increase in land prices. The first part of the table below reveals the magnitude of the increase in the price of land for a new single family home from 1953 to May 1977. It also shows how much the cost of building the house has gone up. The second part makes an adjustment for inflation to show the increase in real terms.

* *Time*, September 12, 1977.
† *Ibid*.

	Median Sales Price of New Home*	House	Land
1953	$11,400	$ 9,473	$ 1,927
May 1977	$49,400	$23,218	$26,182
Percent increase	333%	145%	1,259%

	Adjusted for Inflation		
1953	$11,400	$ 9,473	$ 1,927
May 1977	$22,353	$10,506	$11,847
Percent increase	96%	11%	514%

* National Association of Home Builders.

Although the price increase for the land and house together has been dramatic, we can see that the major factor has been the price of land. As impressive as the above figures are, there are many reasons to believe that the demand for land, and thus its price, will be lessening in the immediate future. As pointed out in the previous chapter, an early peak in the demand from the postwar generation will affect the price of houses. It will also affect the price of land. However, even if such a dramatic peak does not arrive for many years, there are other indications that land may not remain as valuable as it is today.

Investors who believe that land prices will continue to act as a support for housing prices reason that, as a commodity in limited supply, land will inevitably become more valuable as the population increases. However, a brief look at the long-term performance of land prices shows that this belief is a fantasy.

Year	Land Cost in Current Dollars	United States Population
1890	$747	62,948,000
1900	780	75,995,000
1910	895	91,972,000
1920	1,507	105,711,000
1930	1,038	122,775,000
1940	798	131,669,000
1950	1,061	150,697,000

As this table shows, even with a population nearly 2½ times as great in 1950 as it was in 1890, land prices had increased

91

only slightly. Moreover, if we consider the fact that consumer prices in the years between 1890 and 1950 had *tripled*, it is clear that in real terms the value of land had actually decreased. The reason why land prices will not submit to a straight-line supply-demand equation is very simple. There is simply too much land. There is enough land in the United States for each household to have 40 acres. As John McMahan of Stanford University has written, "On a national basis there is not now, nor has there ever been a physical shortage of land for real estate activities."

Nor is all this land confined to rural areas of the country. According to the 1970 United States Census, only 10 percent of the land contained within our nation's metropolitan areas had been developed. Though this percentage has undoubtedly advanced in the years since 1970, it is obvious that there is still plenty of land. It seems, on the basis of these figures, that accelerating land prices are due to factors other than potential limited supply. We have already mentioned two of these factors: the rapid migration of families to the suburbs and a new brisk level of foreign investment in United States property, which together served to *push* demand *ahead of* supply. Environmental and zoning restrictions have served to slow the rate of land development. But given the absolute abundance of land, it is inevitable that supply and demand will soon begin to fall into parity (just as they did in the Chicago, California, and Florida land booms).

Moreover, there appear to be some striking short-term changes in demand patterns. As suburban America has aged and grown, it has proved not to be immune to urban dilemmas. As more and more people have moved to the suburbs, both crime and pollution have increased. Rapid population growth has strained the resources of many suburban schools and has produced the same overcrowding that has for years afflicted schools in the central cities. Meanwhile, the broad, convenient, and expensive freeways have become congested; commuting has frequently become a nightmare; and the once-placid pastoral country ambience of many suburban communities has succumbed to a numbing sprawl of fast-food restaurants and concrete shopping malls. Most important, of course, suburban land is expensive where it was once relatively cheap. It is often much more expensive today than land within the cities.

Faced with these changes in suburban life, several cities (including Seattle and San Francisco) are attracting residents at the expense of their suburbs. Others (like Detroit and Pittsburgh) seem on the verge of such a reverse migration. In many other cities the flight to the suburbs has slowed considerably.

Much of the capital that has flooded into the U.S. real estate market was derived from oil revenue. Benefiting from cartel prices, oil-producing nations, particularly those in the Mideast, received mind-boggling amounts of foreign currency—currency that *had* to be invested. Much of this money was invested in United States banks, industry and real estate. However, as the oil-producing nations begin to develop and industrialize, more of their capital will be required at home. The huge sums of money that originally went into U.S. investments will be increasingly diverted to these countries' goals of becoming full-fledged industrialized nations. Thus, foreign demand for U.S. real estate will likely decrease in the years ahead.

As for zoning restrictions and excessive regulations, it is difficult to determine at the time of this writing whether they are getting better, are static, or getting worse. There could be a case made that as more people discover how much these regulations and restrictions cost they might soon reverse the trend. But regardless of the trend, the supply of developed land will increase. The reason for this is that most of the requirements did not disallow development, but merely delayed it by the entangling web a developer had to pass through before he could build. Many builders reacted to the increasing demand a few years ago, but because of the additional lead time, the supply of land is just beginning to become available for housing that would normally have been present years earlier to meet demand. That demand was met, but at far higher prices than would otherwise have been necessary. The smaller demand and larger supply in the future will be met too, but at lower prices.

Thus, when we analyze the supply and demand factors affecting land we can see why we have had an unprecedented land boom. As the supply of land increases and the demand for it decreases in the near future, upward-accelerating prices will give way to downward-accelerating prices. The current optimistic growth assumptions will prove to be in error; they will be replaced by negative growth assumptions and much lower prices.

11

Inflation

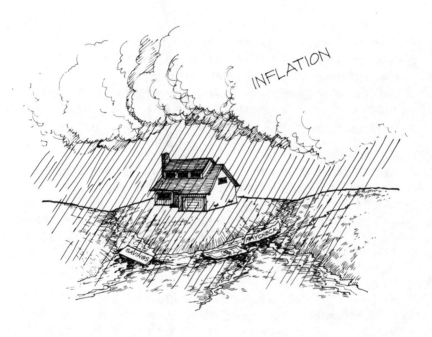

As fortunate as the effects of population trends and land costs have been for real estate, these effects have been matched by the equally fortunate condition of inflation. Why has the generally worrisome and stubborn presence of increasing inflation been good for real estate? For the past two decades, real estate has been one of the best hedges against the shrinking dollar. Reduced to the most basic terms, inflation means that each year our dollars will buy a little less; which in turn means that, if we borrow someone else's dollars, we can pay those dollars back over the years with cheaper ones. The presence of inflation means that if we use leverage to buy something, we can often beat inflation even if the value of what we bought just keeps pace with inflation.* Furthermore, if the inflation *rate* rises, it means that we will not only be paying interest in even cheaper dollars, but we will also find that a mortgage loan itself has increased in value! This increased value occurs because we locked in an interest rate that is lower than can be obtained when there are higher rates of inflation—we borrowed someone else's money when the cost to do so was less. Since real estate investment frequently involves credit that extends over long spans of time, inflation rates have a dynamic effect on leveraged real estate profits and prices.

To illustrate the stimulating effect the presence of increasing inflation has had on real estate profits and prices over the last 10 years, let's see what would have happened had you purchased the average house built in America in 1967, at the then prevailing interest rate.

In 1967 the average new home was selling for approximately $25,000; the perceived rate of inflation was about 2 percent; and the morgage interest rates (which are usually 3 percent above the perceived inflation rate) were around 5 percent. During the 10 years between 1967 and 1977, inflation increased dramatically for several years, at times even entering double digits. Would your investment have kept pace? Let's see.

In 1977 the average existing home was selling for nearly $50,000, a $25,000 increase but an increase that was nearly matched by the increase marked by the consumer price index (which is the standard measure of inflation). If you had paid cash for your house in 1967 you would have a property worth roughly the same in 1977 (in real dollars) as it was in 1967. This is actually no small achievement given the galloping inflation of the period. But you didn't pay cash; you took out a thirty-year mortgage and put 10 percent down.

---

* To illustrate how this happens, suppose you purchased an asset for $10,000 but only put $1,000 into it, borrowing $9,000. If inflation moved the level of prices up 50 percent, and the asset you bought kept pace, it would be worth $15,000. But $15,000 now is worth the same as $10,000 was before inflation. Disregarding interest costs, if you still owed $9,000, your original equity of $1,000 is now worth $6,000 ($15,000 − $9,000). Your $1,000 has increased by 500 percent, beating inflation resoundingly.

96

A few calculations can determine how much profit you have made on the house itself and, in addition, how much you have made on your ever-more-valuable mortgage. (For the purpose of this illustration we will simplify our calculations by ignoring transaction costs, insurance maintenance costs, and rental income or savings.) If, when you sold your house in 1977, you got the average price that 10-year-old houses were attracting in that year, you would have received about $50,000. For 10 years you had been making payments of $120.78 each month. These payments have amounted to $14,494, leaving $18,303 due to be paid over the remaining 20-year life of the loan. Your original down payment was $2,500. By subtracting the $14,494 you have paid, the $18,303 you still owe, and your original $2,500 investment from the $50,000 sale price you show a profit of $14,703, or a 588 percent return over the 10-year period. These figures do not yet include the value of the mortgage you hold, which has 20-years' time remaining. In 1977 the perceived rate of inflation was 6 percent and mortgage interest rates were approximately 9 percent. If your buyer were to take out a new mortgage at these rates, it would mean a monthly payment rate of $164.68, or $39,523 over the next 20 years. Your mortgage, however, required monthly payments of only $120.78, or $28,987 over the remaining 20 years. If your buyer could afford the higher initial investment or could borrow what more was needed elsewhere, his assuming your mortgage would result in a savings of $10,534 distributed over 20 years.

By adding the potential value of your mortgage, your 10-year return swells still further; in fact, the total comes to $25,237, a 1009 percent return on your money in 10 years. Of course, just as the dollars you have been paying have become cheaper due to inflation, your profit has also been paid in cheaper dollars. However, even after we adjust totally for inflation we still show a profit in *real* adjusted dollars of $7,653, or 306 percent. Not only has your investment matched the inflation rate over the last 10 years, you have made a 306 percent *real* profit. These figures illustrate what people mean when they say that real estate is a hedge against inflation. Obviously, an assumption that buying a house now would allow an investor not only to match the inflation rate but actually to provide a profit is a growth assumption. It has, by itself, increased the value of houses. Unfortunately, it is a growth assumption written in air,

97

for the rosy picture that was true in 1967 is simply not true today. Let's return to our $50,000 average house. Were we to have bought an average house in 1977 we would have had to pay an interest rate of about 9 percent (3 percent more than the current 6 percent perceived rate of inflation). We put down 10 percent, or $5,000, and took out a 30-year mortgage for the remaining $45,000. We'll assume, optimistically, that the value of our house will increase at the same rate as inflation in much the same way it did over the previous 10 years.

Annual Inflation Rate From 1977–1987	Real Return Adjusted for Inflation	Percent Return adjusted for Inflation
3%	$ −22,416	−448%
5%	$ −13,741	−275%
6%	$ − 9,933	−199%
7%	$ − 4,838	− 97%
8%	$ − 470	− 9%
9%	$ + 3,230	+ 65%
12%	$ +11,563	+231%
15%	$ +17,287	+346%

Real return over a 10-year period assuming different inflation rates over that period. The inflation rate over that period is assumed to be the perceived inflation rate at the end of the period.

What the table above reveals is that it is an *increasing* rate of inflation that benefits real estate, not the simple existence of inflation in the economy. The table shows that if the inflation rate remained at 6 percent we would lose nearly $10,000 on our investment. In fact, inflation would have to average 9 percent before we would show a profit at all, and would have to average from 12 percent to 15 percent for our profit to match that earned by a homeowner between 1967 and 1977.

Of all the quoted reasons for optimism about the continuing advance of real estate prices, inflation is, probably more than any other condition, seen as a fact of life. Is it? From a historical perspective, assuredly not. Take a look at the following graph. It records price levels in England over the last 1,020 years. Eight hundred and twenty of these years showed relatively stable prices. Any short period of inflation was closely followed by a

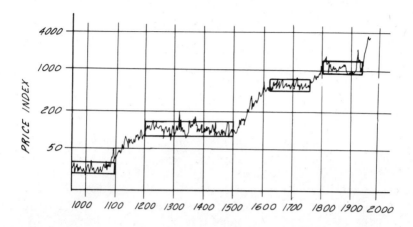

counteracting short period of deflation. Subsequently, however, there were several periods of rapid inflation that, in their
intensity, parallel our own. These periods, lasting anywhere
from 20 to 80 years, saw prices jump to as much as four to five
times their previous levels.

We are in such a period now. Our contemporary bout with
inflation began nearly 40 years ago and has resulted in a quad-
rupling of prices. After four decades of virtually continuous
inflation, it is not surprising that most Americans believe that
the presence of inflation is a fact of life. The English must have
felt similarly in the years 1200, 1600, and 1800. Yet each of these
inflationary eras ended. Will our inflation cycle end similarly?

To answer this question we must take a closer look at what
might have caused the inflationary periods in the past, as well
as what is causing ours today. An article in *Forbes* magazine
(September 15, 1977) observes that each inflationary spiral co-
incided with periods of rapid fundamental changes in England's society and economy. These changes can be outlined like
this:

PERIOD ONE
    New Government: Feudal
    New Economic Sector: Commercial
    New Doctrine: Just Price

PERIOD TWO
New Government: Nation State
New Economic Sector: Capitalist
New Doctrine: Mercantilism

PERIOD THREE
New Government: Democratic State
New Economic Sector: Industrial
New Doctrine: Laissez-faire

PERIOD FOUR
New Government: Bureaucratic State
New Economic Sector: Service
New Doctrine: Mixed Economy

In the last 40 years we have been moving toward a bureau-cratic state. The shift to government by bureaucracy required many adjustments. It also required a lot of money. The newest major sector of our economy is the service sector. The emergence of this new major division within the economy has required expensive adjustments and may be contributing to inflation, as is the equally profound change in economic doctrine from laissez-faire to mixed economy.

These shifts toward a bureaucratic government and a mixed economy, along with the emergence of the dominant service sector, have created social and economic changes as profound as any of the previous changes we've outlined—changes that our graph shows to have inaugurated periods of galloping inflation.

The above graph also indicates that when the changes are complete, inflation cools and deflation can even occur. We might then assume that if the changes that are occurring within our economy are ending, if the metamorphosis is complete, our inflationary period might be ending.

With a taxpayers' revolt in progress across the nation and with political rhetoric consistently bemoaning big government, it would seem that the growth of government bureaucracy may be ending and the shift to a mixed economy is stalled. Although the service sector of our economy is still growing, as our country approaches the 1980s it appears that the era of rapid fundamental change is ending. As it ends, history suggests that the inflationary cycle will once again fade.

As the next graph shows, our own economy has experienced the same trends as Britain's over the last 100 years. You'll note that from 1870 through 1901 prices were in decline, indicating deflation. After the turn of the century a slight inflationary trend developed. Then, beginning in 1914, there was a five-year expansion in prices. In this period prices rose 100 percent, which is a 15 percent annual rate of inflation (15 percent compounded annually produces a 100 percent gain in five years). After 1919 we experienced a period of general deflation until 1932. From 1932 to 1940 the inflation rate hovered near zero, only to increase 74 percent during the next seven years. Deflation set in again in 1947 and lasted two years.

CONSUMER PRICE INDEX
1967 = 100

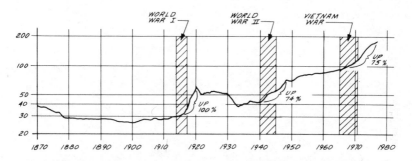

Our current period of inflation began in 1949, though for the first 15 years the inflation rate averaged less than 2 percent annually. In 1965, however, the pace began to quicken. From 1965 to 1975 prices again advanced 75 percent, while the annual rate of inflation peaked in 1974 at 12.2 percent.

Two periods of actual deflation occurred a few years after both world wars. Since during the Vietnam War and its winding down we experienced wartime inflation, we might experience deflation soon. Even if the inflation rate should stay the same or go somewhat higher it will be negative for real estate, as shown in the table on page 98. If inflation begins to abate, as the evidence indicates it probably will, it will be even more negative for real estate. Should the years ahead bring a period of deflation, the real estate market will be a total disaster.

101

12

Taxation

While inflation has pushed up real estate prices, it has also pushed up the tax burden for the average American. As incomes went up with inflation and pushed people into higher and higher tax brackets, the tax bite became increasingly larger. The tax treatment of real estate has been about the same for decades, but since the late '60s this treatment has offered increasingly larger benefits as incomes increased with inflation.

For homeowners the deduction of mortgage interest has made a house a tax shelter as well as a place to live. Most feel renting is like throwing money down the drain.

Favored tax treatment has prompted millions of people to purchase additional real estate for the tax shelter value. Although inflated prices usually do not permit a current income and often cause monthly cash losses as high mortgage payments and expenses exceed rental receipts, investor enthusiasm has not been deterred since these expenses have been fully deductible.

Buying $200,000 worth of real estate, for example, using $20,000 down and $180,000 in mortgages at 9 percent for 30 years allows $155,000 in tax write-offs over 10 years from the mortgage interest alone. Moreover, the "points" charged on the loan (one point is one percent of the mortgage loan) have also been deductible in the first year of purchase. Two points on $200,000 of real estate allows a $3,600 deduction immediately. In some areas five points and more are charged.

Straight-line depreciation also offers additional tax write-offs on investment property. And unlike most other forms of investment, the straight-line depreciation taken in the past is not taxable as ordinary income when the property is sold for more than its depreciated value. Depreciating $200,000 of real estate over 25 years on a straight-line basis generates $8,000 in annual tax write-offs. When the property is sold these write-offs are taxed as a capital gain, which is generally one-half the rate on ordinary income.

The Revenue Act of 1978 further increased tax benefits for real estate. For taxpayers 55 and older, up to $100,000 in profits from the sale of a personal residence is not taxed. This one-time exemption is allowed provided the residence is owned and occupied by the seller for at least three years out of five immediately preceding the sale. Previously, individuals had to be 65 years old and could exclude all profits if the sale price was under $35,000 and a portion of the gain if the sale price exceeded that amount. A provision that allows all homeowners to trade up within 18 months after selling a principal residence and defer capital gains taxes still remains in effect. Now younger homeowners can trade up, pyramiding boom-time profits until they are 55, and avoid a large tax bite altogether.

Accelerated depreciation was also used to generate much larger write-offs, and if the property was held long enough, even the excess over straight-line could be taxed at the preferential capital gains rate when sold.

Lax standards allowed vacation homes to be treated as investments offering the same tax benefits even if they were used primarily by their owners.

With the tax benefits curtailed on most other forms of investment since the late '60s (by the 1969 Tax Reform Act in particular), and with tax bites increasing for the average American, investors by the millions have been taking advantage of the generous tax treatment of real estate.

Although at this writing real estate still retains favorable tax treatment as an investment vehicle, the mood in Washington appears to be changing, as evidenced by the 1976 Tax Reform Act and the Revenue Act of 1978.

The overriding objective of current tax-reform thinking is economic neutrality. This means that one form of investment should not be favored over others. Thus, corporations and individuals should not invest in oil, cattle feeding, timber, or real estate simply because these areas are taxed at lower rates. This will, of course, require tightening the tax laws and plugging the "loopholes."

Tightening the tax laws will also conform with prevailing understanding of tax justice. Popular sentiment is that the rich exploit tax shelters and don't pay their fair share, while those in the middle-income group bear the cost of government. By plugging tax loopholes Congress feels that it will be promoting economic neutrality and efficiency as well as tax justice.

The Tax Reform Act of 1976 is clear evidence of this prevailing trend. One significant restriction is a much lower limit on the amount of investment-interest expense that can be deducted. An investor buying $200,000 of income property showing an even cash flow, with mortgages totalling $180,000 at 9 percent for 30 years, can no longer deduct all of the interest expense. Only $10,000 of the first year's interest expense of $16,120 can be deducted. If the cash flow remains the same over the next 10 years, only $100,000 of interest will be allowed as a deduction, which is $55,000 less than the previous amount. Moreover, the points that are paid can no longer be deducted in the first year. This expense must now be spread over the life of the mortgage. Two points paid on a mortgage of $180,000 will be a deduction of $120 instead of $3,600 in the first year. Other restrictions specify that the depreciation in excess of straight-line is now taxable as ordinary income regardless of the holding period upon disposition. The regulations regarding vacation homes are now quite strict. There are many other tax benefits that have been removed by the 1976 Tax Reform Act and, since it appears that very few people are aware of them, we have included most of them in Appendix A.

Although the Revenue Act of 1978 increased the lifetime exemption for older homeowners, it provided benefits for other investments that are more significant. The capital gains tax was lowered across the board, which increases the incentive for investment in other areas previously out of the tax-favored arena. The corporate tax rate was reduced substantially, which directly raises corporate profitability and earnings, making stocks a better investment as well as increasing the incentive for capital formation. The act also lowered individual income tax rates and increased tax deductions in a variety of areas. The overall effect lowers the tax burden of the average American and promotes economic neutrality—a boon to investments other than real estate.

In addition to the firm evidence provided by the Tax Reform Act of 1976 and the Revenue Act of 1978, the prevailing trend away from favorable tax status for real estate is further evidenced by suggestions from the Carter Administration that there be a ceiling on the amount of mortgage interest homeowners can deduct on their residences. The reasoning behind this is that the mortgage-interest deduction is a tax break only for the upper-income levels since these are generally the people with houses. The mortgage-interest deduction is viewed as another loophole available only to the upper strata of society, which, therefore, contradicts the major objective behind the current tax reform.

Whether or not a limitation will be put on a homeowner's mortgage-interest deduction is a moot point. With home prices at such inflated levels, this deduction no longer makes owning a home cheaper than renting in most metropolitan areas. It is quite typical, for example, to find $100,000 homes that can be

105

rented for $500 a month or less. Considering the expenses in owning a house, such as mortgage payments, insurance, property taxes, and maintenance, for taxpayers, including those in the highest brackets, it is cheaper to rent than to buy, even with all the tax advantages intact.

Another loophole that will undoubtedly be coming to the attention of Congress is the treatment of straight-line depreciation on investment property. With other forms of investment, write-offs generated through the use of straight-line depreciation are taxable as ordinary income when sold. Currently, this write-off is taxed as a capital gain on disposition. This favorable tax treatment is not likely to be consistent with current tax-reform thinking.

Exactly when and to what extent the remaining tax advantages will be removed from real estate is hard to say, but the trend is clear. The 1976 Tax Reform Act and the Revenue Act of 1978 removed, or are in the process of removing, many benefits once enjoyed exclusively by real estate investors. There undoubtedly will be more restrictions ahead. This trend will be realized by investors, with a depressing effect on prices.

13

Proposition 13

So far we have discussed fundamentals that have been acting on real estate for some time: population, land, inflation, taxation. In June of 1978, a new development in California sparked the attention of real estate owners across the country. It was the passage of the Jarvis-Gann Initiative, more popularly known as Proposition 13.

Proposition 13 set the maximum property tax rate at one percent of the 1975–1976 county assessors' valuations. When improvements are made or the property changes ownership, the current appraised value is used in determining the one percent maximum. Once a value is set on the property, it cannot increase by more than 2 percent in any given year. In addition, the amendment requires a two-thirds vote of the California legislature to increase any state taxes and a two-thirds vote of the registered voters in any locality to impose any new local taxes. The passage of Proposition 13 gave California property owners an average reduction of 57 percent in their property taxes. Moreover, the voting requirement made it more difficult to increase state and local taxes.

Since lowering property taxes reduces the cost of owning a home, the effect of Proposition 13 will be positive for the real estate market. Prior to Proposition 13, the California property taxes on a $100,000 house averaged roughly $2,000. After the amendment, taxes dropped to some $860. This rollback means an annual tax savings of $1,140 and makes the house much more affordable. Of course reducing the cost of owning a home will stimulate new demand for houses, and as new demand hits the market, prices will increase and the trade-up market will be stimulated as well.

Although Proposition 13 is confined to California, a movement to cut property taxes is spreading across the country. Shortly after California's vote a national Associated Press –NBC News poll revealed 75 percent of the American public felt property taxes were too high and should be lowered, even at the expense of government services. Within six weeks, 30 states had similar amendments under consideration, and Howard Jarvis had invitations to campaign in 40 states. With a wave of property-tax cutting moving across the country, stimulating new demand for houses, the effect on the national real estate market will be positive. But for homeowners, the situation is more cloudy.

Homeowners' tax savings, for instance, will be smaller than it might first appear. Since property taxes are deductions on state and federal income taxes, the reduction will result in an increase in other taxes. Californians, on the average, will return 37 percent of their savings to the state and federal governments. Not only are property tax savings smaller than they might first appear, but it is dangerous for homeowners to assume these savings will translate into a lasting increase in the prices of their homes. In California, as in most metropolitan areas across the country, the frenzied real estate market has pushed prices into an emotional spiral beyond reason. Using the positive effect of lower property taxes as a reason to buy real estate is like paying five times too much for a television set that suddenly comes with a free stand.

Proposition 13 has spawned further political agitation that will insure any buying spree is short-lived. By lowering property taxes, the amendment gave real estate investors who rent out their property windfall profits. But this was not the drafters' intention. Their intent was to provide savings to homeowners and renters alike. Co-author Howard Jarvis has begun campaigning to insure these profits are returned to renters in the form of rent reductions. Joining him in this campaign is his former foe, Governor Jerry Brown. Once vehemently opposed to Proposition 13, Brown performed a political pirouette after its passage and is now on the rent-cutting campaign trail with his "good buddy," Howard Jarvis. In a Los Angeles press conference, Brown said there would be "inexorable pressures [for rent controls] if the apartment owners don't shape up. . . . There's enough political energy in this state to make these laws spring up like a thousand flowers from San Diego to Eureka." Of course the mere possibility of rent controls is enough to upset the real estate market and affect investors and homeowners alike. While the possibility of rent controls is unsettling, a look at the politics of Proposition 13 discloses more problems for real estate.

Proposition 13 was passed by a 2-to-1 margin in the face of predicted cutbacks in police protection, fire protection, schools, libraries, and employment. Without waiting to see the extent of damage such a drastic measure will cause in California, other states have followed immediately with similar propositions. Why? Clearly the majority of Americans don't trust government and they want less of it. They are tired of paying so much in taxes for the benefits they receive. They want lower taxes. Two days after Proposition 13 passed, U.S. Senate Majority Leader Robert Byrd summed it up: "It reflects the general concern about inflation and the need for a tax cut. . . ."

A tax cut may be possible if the government reacts to pressure from the public to reduce spending and balance the budget. With inflation now considered to be our greatest public problem the government already feels public pressure to reduce spending and deficits. A balanced budget is of course a major objective of the Carter Administration. Proposition 13 and the burgeoning tax revolt will help them in this task substantially. Since property taxes are deductions on federal income taxes, reduced property taxes mean federal income tax deductions will decline, and incoming budget revenues will increase.

Proposition 13 reduced Californians' property taxes and thus federal tax deductions by $7 billion. This means increased tax revenues to the federal government of some $2.3 billion from California residents alone. As the movement spreads and other states cut property taxes, revenues to the federal government could rise to $20 billion or more, a major slice of the current $50 billion deficit. Thus, the task of lowering federal deficits and lowering federal taxes will become much easier as a result of the taxpayers revolt.

Consider the effect on real estate prices should the government succeed in reducing the deficit and cutting taxes.

Not only would reduced government spending have a dampening effect on inflation, but an accompanying tax cut is also a potent inflation fighter. To illustrate why lowering taxes lowers the cost of goods and services let's look at a cake you buy in your local supermarket. What makes this cake cost what it does? Its basic ingredients, eggs, milk, flour, sugar, come from various producers. To supply these ingredients producers have expenses—one of which is taxes. Paying taxes is also a cost to the middlemen: the grain elevators, mills, railroads, bakers, truckers, clerks, sales people, supermarkets. A cake pays a lot of taxes! All businesses involved must make enough profit to maintain their existence and function. Since they all pay taxes on income, they must charge enough for their services or products to pay those taxes. Lowering taxes will, of course, lower the cost of cake. Since lowering taxes will reduce the cost of all goods and services, the inflation rate will decline.

Lowering property taxes will have the same effect. Shortly after Proposition 13 was passed, the Federal Budget Office estimated the reduction of property taxes in California alone will reduce the nation's inflation rate by 0.2 percent in 1978 and by 0.4 percent in 1979. As other states join in property tax cuts, the impact on inflation will multiply.

Besides having a deflationary effect, a tax cut will cause further difficulties for real estate. A prime incentive for investing in real estate has come from its tax shelter value. As income tax

110

burdens decline, the need for a tax shelter will diminish and a large source of demand will dissipate.

Thus, it appears the tax revolt inaugurated by Proposition 13 has negative implications for real estate. Remember from our discussion on inflation and the table on page 98 that only an increase in the inflation rate provides real gains in real estate. Obviously, a decline in the rate of inflation will be disastrous. So will rent regulation and the diminishing need for tax shelters.

14

The Business Cycle and the Boom Cycle

There is one looming, cyclical occurrence that always unsettles real estate investors and home buyers. At regular intervals the country undergoes a period of tight money, or a "credit crunch"—a time when interest rates skyrocket. Credit becomes expensive—so expensive that it is impractical to obtain a mortgage. Since a credit crunch can cause a decline in real estate prices, it has become a focal point of concern.

In four-year cycles, 1966, '70, and '74, interest rates rose sharply and money became tight, causing a credit crunch. These recurring periods are spawned by the business cycle, which periodically takes the economy from a recession to a credit crunch. It can be diagramed as follows:

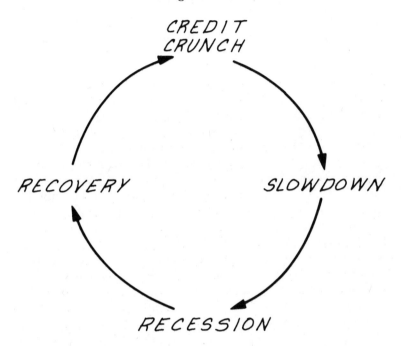

During a recession business is soft. Because the demand for financing is low, interest rates are also low. But as memories of the recession grow dim, consumers gain confidence and spending increases. Healthy business conditions are refueled by this growing confidence, causing an upward spiral. Should this spiral continue unchecked, consumer demand would exceed supply, but there is a natural restraint. As consumer demand increases, so does the demand for credit, resulting in abnormally high interest rates. Credit becomes expensive. Since mortgage-interest rates are high, home building declines, causing construction-related unemployment. These unemployed people defer their spending which affects all sectors of the economy. Luxury industries are the first to be hit as people postpone vacations and make do with last year's Cadillac. Like a wave, recession moves on and ripples over other industries such as apparel, appliances, and furniture. As it passes through the economy, the wave caused by high interest rates aggravates unemployment and lowers consumer demand. As a result, a new recession is born and the cycle starts again.

Thus, the business cycle. During times of tight money, mortgage lending dries up, real estate buying is deferred and, in many cases, real estate values decline, causing investor consternation.*

Consternation, however, is mild in comparison to the devastation generated by a major real estate crash. The boom-bust forces are much more powerful and dynamic than those of the business cycle. Once a boom is in force it is unlikely that current business conditions will turn it around.

In 1970, for example, in the midst of the apartment boom, there was a severe credit crunch, the most disrupting since the early 1920s. Yet the apartment boom survived. And though the credit crunch of 1974 added severity to the already crashing apartment market, the housing boom was building steam and home prices actually increased that year. The boom-bust cycle is more powerful and dominates its weaker relative, the business cycle. Thus we find the fear of the cyclical credit crunch is overdramatized and unwarranted. The focal point of concern should not be on the business cycle but on the powerful and destructive boom-bust cycle.

A boom has a life of its own and thus a cycle of its own. It operates like the business cycle, but on a much longer, more powerful, and larger scale. Money is drawn into a boom in tremendous amounts, and the use of credit expands enormously. Leverage becomes commonplace. Down payments become razor thin, allowing financing of 90 percent and more. Each marginal price increase produces tenfold profits and more. These profits, when leveraged again, increase holdings greatly. Debt increases at a faster rate than prices. The boom feeds on itself, fueled largely by speculative pyramiding. During the maturing stages of the boom, the demand for financing becomes insatiable and the interest rates soar.

---

* It will be interesting to see what happens in 1979 since savings and loans can now get money through Treasury Bill six-month accounts.

At this point, prices are extremely vulnerable and history shows the end is near. When the cost of financing climbs to prohibitive levels a credit crunch of the highest order exists. The paper superstructure soon collapses.

During the stock market boom of the 1920s, brokers' loans were expanding in the billions. Ten percent down on stock purchases was common. From 1918 to 1929, brokers' loans climbed at the annual compound rate of 13.7 percent while the Dow Jones Industrial Average rose at a lesser rate of 13 percent. In March 1929, the interest rate on brokers' loans peaked at a lofty 20 percent. The crash followed within six months.

We can see the same progression in today's inflated housing market. In 1944 mortgage debt stood at $17.9 billion. Over the past 10 years mortgage debt increased sharply, expanding to more than $560 billion through 1977. This is an annual compounded increase of better than 16 percent since 1944. Meanwhile, prices have climbed only 8.71 percent compounded annually. Clearly the increase in debt has well outpaced the increase in prices.

Prior to 1975 mortgage interest rates moved up and down with the pulsating business cycle. Since then, however, a frightening deviation has developed. As a result of the 1974–1975 recession, interest rates dropped and the cost of most forms of financing became cheaper through 1976. Ordinarily, mortgage rates should have come down sharply. But they didn't. In most localities they declined only marginally, if at all, due to the ravenous demand for financing, a definite sign the boom is maturing. At this writing mortgage rates have reached 10 percent. Such speculative mortgage demand can and will be choked by prohibitive financing rates. The housing boom is entering its own tight-money period, a credit crunch that marks the beginning of the end. Unlike the ephemeral ripples caused by the business cycle, this credit crunch will generate a tidal wave, powerful enough to drown the real estate market and swamp the entire economy.

15

Recap

In our analysis of today's housing boom we have examined what investors are seeing and, more important, what they are not seeing. We have noted the emergence of several primary reasons to invest in real estate, and we have found reason to doubt the absolute faith placed in all of these reasons by investors. But even if all these reasons for investing in real property were to remain strong, or even strengthen, it would not deter the coming crash. The crash is coming because of what is not being widely seen: that is, speculation, rapid expansion of growth assumptions and premiums, and the omnipresent marketplace reality-anticipation.

When a boom becomes a boom, it develops a life of its own. Optimistic thinking leads to growth assumptions, and once a growth assumption is present, a spiral begins. Speculation increases, prices rise, and growth assumptions expand still further. This is the price spiral we illustrated with our missile example.

We have found in our historical examples that the peaks of booms occur when optimism is at its highest. As boomsters toasted the opening of the Illinois-Michigan Canal, prices broke. Florida's land prices plummeted even as flivvers by the thousands were still putt-putting down the Dixie Highway. Stock prices broke in 1929 in the midst of raging optimism about America's "new era of prosperity." In each of these cases, and in every other case we have studied, what happened was that prices simply anticipated the optimism of the time. From that point on the market finds itself in the deadly boom cycle where prices are going up because they are going up. Each price rise triggers a new assumption of further growth. As this acceleration continues, prices advance far beyond any level the original optimistic conditions would have supported. When that happens, as we saw in our missile flight, the crash is inevitable.

A brief conversation about real estate at a party or at a place of work will almost always focus on the one real reason why people are optimistic about the continued price performance of their real estate. They will give you figures, tell you how much their home has increased in value, tell you tales they heard from a real estate broker about future price increases. After only a few minutes of this it will be clear that the major reason for investing in real estate today is the popular perception that prices are going to continue to go up, a perception that is grounded only in the fact that prices are going up now. When you hear this you will know that the price spiral is underway and, for investors, this price spiral is a ticking bomb.

Part Four

The Crash

16

The Beginning of the Crash

Part of the anatomy of a boom is the anatomy of a crash. We saw its stages in our hypothetical missile flight: a fierce, emotionally inspired acceleration, a slight decline in the rate of price acceleration, a leveling of prices, a slight decline in prices, and then the rapid, downward spiraling price decline that marks a crash in the public mind. In several of our historical examples, these stages were passed through so quickly that they were obscured by the general panic that surrounded plunging prices; in others, the intermediate stages before and after the price peak were more prolonged and were later explained by hopeful, though futile, claims that the market was merely experiencing a "healthy breathing spell." No matter how quickly these stages occurred, however, they were always a part of every crash. There is always a period of rapid price increases, a period when the rate of price increases slows, and a stage where they stop, or fluctuate up and down going nowhere. This stage then deteriorates into a small decline in price levels, and finally price collapse. However, the early stages are often not recognized because of the euphoria associated with the peak of a boom.

Most historians place the start of the Great Stock Market Crash at Black Tuesday, October 29, 1929. We, however, saw that the crash actually began nearly two months before Black Tuesday, when the continuous price increases stopped and daily changes became volatile both upward and downward. Stocks continued to crash for three years after Black Tuesday. In 1929, as in every major boom our country has experienced, the subtle, dangerous early changes in the mood of the market were not noticed because, except for some occasional short breathing spells, prices had been rising for years and optimism was high. This refusal to submit to cautious pessimism in the midst of a boom is understandable. It is also tragic, for these subtle early changes in the character of the market are often the only early warning that boomtime investors are given. Just as with all past booms, today's housing boom is coming to an end. The same subtle early changes that have presaged catastrophic price declines in the past have begun to appear in today's real estate market. Even if the crash evolves slowly and the changes take place over many months, or even years, nonetheless the evidence points to the inescapable conclusion that the early stages of the crash have begun.

According to the National Association of Realtors, the median price of an existing home increased at an annual rate of 20.5 percent in the first quarter of 1977 and accelerated even more in the second quarter, the rate increasing to 23.4 percent. But in the third quarter these brisk advances evaporated. The third quarter growth rate was only 3.7 percent. This ominous trend continued as the year closed at an annual growth rate of 3.6 percent. Prices were still increasing, but the rate of increase had fallen so sharply that by the beginning of 1978 it no longer even matched the inflation rate, which at that time was calculated at 6.8 percent. This meant that, in adjusted terms, people were actually experiencing a real decline in the value of their houses during the months of July through December 1977.*

Meanwhile the Commerce Department reported that the average selling price of a new home actually declined during one three-month period in 1977 (July through September); while in some local markets even sharper declines were reported. San Jose, in the midst of California's booming Santa Clara Valley, saw a $6,000 drop in the price of an average house in the month of August alone. This amounted to a full 10 percent drop in one month, and it alerted investigators to the surprising fact that housing prices had actually been in decline at more modest rates months before. The graph below shows more recent figures for the entire state of California. These figures, of course, do not prove that a catastrophic decline is occurring in national housing prices, for such a decline is clearly not happening . . . yet. What they do indicate is a change in the mood of the market. The strong bull market in real estate, whose prices had pushed inexorably ahead month after month with only the most infrequent local declines, has shifted to a more nervously complected, speculative market whose larger monthly shifts, both upward and downward, are being recorded.

The figures in the graphs on page 125 are national compilations averaging local areas, some of which are rising and some of which are declining. Most local prices are actually more volatile. Unfortunately this volatility is hard to see. Unlike the stock

* The first three quarters of 1978 saw some down months for existing homes, but the annual rate of increase was 20.8 percent, 16.4 percent, and 14.8 percent respectively.

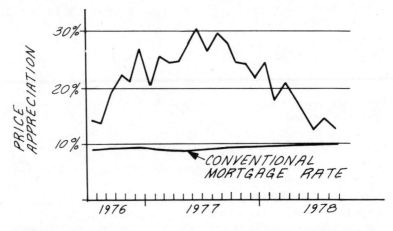

CALIFORNIA HOUSING
(YEAR TO YEAR CHANGE)

PRICE APPRECIATION

30%

20%

10%

CONVENTIONAL MORTGAGE RATE

1976　　　1977　　　1978

The median price of a home in California was $71,452 in August 1978, up only 12.7% from a year earlier. Meanwhile, interest rates climbed from 9% to 10%. The trends continued through September and October. **Source:** *Forbes Magazine.*

market, whose combined averages can be seen at a glance, the compilation of real estate market statistics is a complex, painstaking, and time-consuming operation. If your stock account or savings account were to drop in value tomorrow by $5,000, you would know it very quickly. But if the value of a house you own were to drop by $5,000, it would likely be months before you could learn of the decline . . . if you knew where to look. Even when the figures are compiled, they are difficult to obtain these days. When we went to our local board of realtors to get housing-price figures for our area we were told that they do not provide information on price changes to the general public. This reticence was a distinct change from the early, much more bullish months of 1977 when such figures often arrived in one's mailbox unbidden, in flyers from local realtors.

Once it becomes apparent to many people that real estate values are softening (perhaps six months to a year after the fact) the market will then begin its long slide toward crash, though

NEW HOME PRICES
(MEDIAN)

EXISTING HOME PRICES
(MEDIAN)

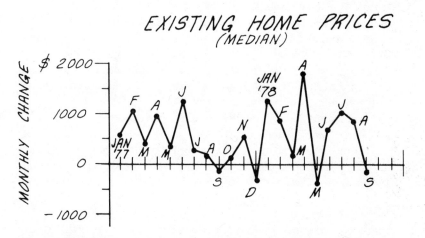

These graphs indicate the upward and downward volality of the national real estate market. The figures show the change in the monthly median price. **Sources:** The National Association of Home Builders and the National Association of Realtors.

the slide will probably not be steady but will have encouraging recoveries along the way.

As real estate values register a decline, many home buyers will likely see it as a fleeting opportunity to buy real estate at attractive levels. Real estate brokers will likely fuel enthusiasm for these bargains at slightly lower prices by selling "last chance" concepts to buyers. The "healthy breathing spell" in the superheated real estate market will be described as normal.

There will probably be enough demand left at these slightly lower prices to cause real estate values to rise again—for a while. But the next time the market goes up some speculators will have been shaken. Their greed will be tempered with fear. Some will sell. Other speculators will not buy, waiting to see if there is another decline. And some potential panic buyers seeing that prices have actually come down will feel less urgency to buy a house before the need arises. Banks and savings and loans may reassess their lending policies.

Bargain hunters will probably get things going again, but the slight shift in supply-demand factors will cut this advance in prices short, and real estate values will again begin to drop.

There will likely be more "healthy breathing spells" but each one will shake confidence a little more. They will become more frequent and extended.

Speculators holding on through the ups and downs will become impatient; they will be more willing to rent their houses out at low prices to cushion the blow of negative cash flow. This will bring rents down and more people will decide to rent at these bargain rates rather than buy a house. Thus, the decline will become more pronounced as there are fewer buyers, and as real estate values decline, many more speculators will be forced by fear or necessity to sell.

The more real estate declines, the more the word will spread. What's left of speculative buying will diminish rapidly. Those buyers who previously might have bought a home even though it was unnecessary, and potential panic buyers who might have bought though they couldn't really afford it, will be leaving the market. Now folks will begin *waiting* to buy in order to get better prices, reversing a trend that has persisted for three decades. Thus, the decline itself will remove a tremendous demand factor.

126

What will have vanished from the market is a sense of urgency. The supply of houses for sale will increase. Home builders will have wrestled many new houses through the mesh of regulations and restrictions. Suddenly some people will have *lost* money in real estate.

It might seem that as prices decline demand will increase as new people who have less money enter the market, but this will not be the case. Here's why. Let's assume a prospective buyer goes down to his friendly bank or savings and loan for a mortgage. Our buyer wants a home that will cost $60,000, down $15,000 from its boom price. The loan officer works for an institution whose wealth is based on declining real estate which they have as collateral and is much more reluctant to make a loan. Instead of 10 to 20 percent down, 30 to 40 percent is required. The property will be appraised much more conservatively, and lending restrictions will increase. New regulations will likely require that the home cost less than two times our buyer's gross income as opposed to the three times gross that was the boomtime rule. Mortgage interest rates will be higher because there is very little money available to lend on real estate that is not going up. Thus, as prices decline our buyer will find the $60,000 house harder to buy than the $75,000 house is today.

Because of the shrinking amounts of leverage banks and savings and loans will allow, and the general unavailability of money to loan on real estate, prices will have to fall a great deal before any demand is sparked by people who are finally able to afford the houses they could not afford at boom prices. You can see how subtle these changes might be. They will add uncertainty to a market that was once a sure-fire path to riches. As we saw in our historical exhibits, there is a limit to how many "healthy breathing spells" can be declared before public confidence is shaken, and even a slight loss in public confidence will have its effect.

These, then, are the leveling forces that will be acting on prices as the crash enters its second early stage: the abandonment of real estate by nervous or overextended speculators, increasing caution by lending institutions, the disappearance of panic buying, the increase in supply of houses for sale by builders. These leveling forces will be more than enough to

127

send prices into a spiraling decline. Let's freeze the declining spiral momentarily at 20 percent down to visualize how various individuals and institutions might react at this point.

The most volatile constituent of our boom is self-described speculators, the folks who are trying to turn $5,000 into a fortune in their spare time. These speculators have tried to become millionaires by "pyramiding" their holdings. For instance, a speculator may have bought a house a few years ago for $50,000 by putting 10 percent down; another house in the next year for $60,000, again 10 percent down; and yet another house a year later for $70,000. This third house might have required a 20 percent down payment, but it was easily obtained by taking out second mortgages or refinancing houses one and two. All three houses were worth $70,000 before the decline. Our speculator put up $5,000 to purchase the first house, $6,000 for the second house, and then used the appreciation on both of these houses to finance the third. The figures are attractive. An $11,000 investment has in two years produced an equity of $41,000 in property with a market value of $210,000. This is an increase in equity of $30,000, a healthy 272 percent in two years.

But with a decline in prices of 20 percent, our speculator's silver lining very quickly disappears. The decline has trimmed $14,000 off the potential sale price of each of the houses. Together they are now worth $168,000. The mortgage loans amount to $169,000. If forced to sell, our speculator will not only have lost that attractive $41,000 in equity, and the original $11,000 investment, but will end up a further $1,000 in the red. Transaction costs and a monthly negative cash flow will make his situation worse. This is certainly a less-than-enjoyable way of spending one's spare time.

It should be noted that the speculator in this hypothetical example is in a very safe position compared to many, if not most, speculators who are active in today's real estate markets. In California and other hyperactive markets across the country, our hapless speculator would be dismissed as a mere dabbler. We have talked to many speculators of relatively modest means who own 25 or more houses. Due to normal expenses, some of these folks report that they are now forced to sell a house or two a year just to make ends meet.

No one knows how much of the nation's housing stock is

128

currently in the hands of speculators. Estimates range as high as 40 percent in some areas. Undoubtedly some speculators have adequate outside assets to weather a downturn like this one, but it is also clear that for many highly leveraged speculators a 20 percent dip in prices may spell the difference between being a paper millionaire and being very much broke. At any rate, it is clear that a 20 percent decline in prices would spark, through uneasiness and foreclosure, a massive new wave of houses for sale.

Besides this class of speculators, homes in America are owned by people who purchased them with no speculative intent whatsoever. These folks will, in general, be much more able to weather a 20 percent downturn in prices. Still, we must divide these homeowners into two distinct groups, for one group is in a much more exposed position than the other.

As we have previously stated, people who buy in a speculative market are to some extent speculators no matter what their intentions. Most people who purchased homes during the boom years fall into this category. They include people who felt they should buy a house because they heard it was a good investment as well as a place to live; people who figured, given relatively loose credit requirements, that they could buy as cheaply as they could rent; and the previously cited panic buyers who rushed to buy a home before it was too late. Let's assume a family that falls into this category of homeowner bought a house a few years ago for $60,000. Because they were a bit more cautious than most speculators, they put down 20 percent of the sale price and didn't take out a second mortgage. As prices went up, this family's home eventually reached $70,000. Now, however, that price has been eroded by 20 percent and is only worth $56,000. They have lost $4,000 but still have $8,000 in equity. If they were forced to sell they would have to absorb a loss, but not a serious one. They are making payments of $400 a month (not including insurance and property taxes), but if they were to sell they would have to live somewhere else. So even with a 20 percent decline, these folks would apparently have no reason to sell.

The effect of the price decline on this family would be the loss of security and money represented by the devalued sale price and their eroded equity. When their house was worth

$70,000, our family, if they were to suffer a financial setback such as a loss of job or an extended illness, could have gone to a bank, a savings and loan, or a mortgage loan company where a second mortgage or other refinancing plan could have produced their accumulated equity.

But with the shrinkage of equity, our family, and millions like them, will find that their financial position has become much more tenuous. Inevitably, some of these folks will be forced by random economic hardship to sell their homes. Others will sell in an attempt to consolidate their debt situations. In either case, this class of homeowners will contribute a new fund of houses to an already depressed market.

The class of real estate owners who will least feel the price dip are those folks who have anywhere from 50 percent to 100 percent equity in the homes that they bought early on when the housing boom began. (Other homeowners in this category are more recent homebuyers who have substantial non-real-estate-related assets.) The equity of these homeowners will decline substantially in value and they will suffer a real loss of money; and though they can take some consolation in the fact that the devaluation of their property may at least result in lower property taxes and insurance rates, their loss of equity would dwarf any such savings.

These two large groups of relatively secure homeowners will not immediately contribute much to a declining market, but the houses sold by other more vulnerable owners will have a profound effect on the real estate market and the institutions that service it.

Banks, savings and loans, and mortgage loan companies will be going through some tough times, but they have experienced similar credit crunches many times before as a result of the business cycle. They will look at their current problems as temporary and project that better times are around the corner. Home builders will be reacting similarly. There will be layoffs, and building permits will be dropping. Builders will be holding unsold houses, but like the financial institutions, they have seen slumps before and will be looking for housing demand to pick up soon.

17

The Crash

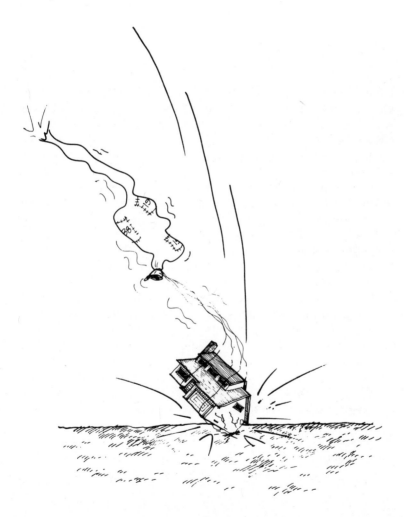

In the previous chapter we visualized what it would be like when real estate values had declined a moderate 20 percent in value. Up to that point few Americans would be concerned or even aware of the decline. As we have seen, however, individuals and institutions will be reacting to the subtly changing market in real estate even though they are not fully aware of their motivations.

We will now move forward in time to see why real estate, after its "breathing spell," will not be ready for a new advance, but rather for a devastating decline far below the 20 percent level we just depicted.

In terms of public participation, the housing boom that we have experienced over the last few years dwarfs all of the booms we have examined. Today, two-thirds of the families in America own their own homes compared to fewer than a third in Florida and elsewhere during the 1920s. The percentage of Americans who actually held stock during the great crash of 1929 was far smaller. Furthermore, the amount of money involved in today's housing market is so vast as to be unimaginable. In 1978 the boom had boosted the value of single family dwellings in the United States to $2.1 trillion. The outstanding mortgage debt was roughly $600 billion, which indicates an equity figure of $1.5 trillion. An idea of the size of this nearly incomprehensible figure can be gained from the fact that it would be sufficient to wipe out all consumer debt in this country with enough spare change to eliminate the national debt as well.

Because of this vast participation in real estate, millions of Americans will gradually become aware that real estate is declining. Some may begin to doubt what a generation has taught—that real estate will always go up. Many will become concerned.

As real estate values continue to shrink and the decline becomes acknowledged, speculators and homeowners will react in significant numbers by selling. Lending institutions will react with more restrictive lending policies. Home builders may try to hold on to their inventory of unsold housing. But many will have to sell in order to meet overdue construction loans.

With the actions of these individuals and institutions adding

132

to the supply and subtracting from the demand, housing prices will spiral downward. The trend wll not be easily reversed. As the crash deepens, its effect on market participants will be sharper.

As we have pointed out, the most volatile constituent in the boom was the self-described speculators. As noted in the example of the speculator with three houses on page 128, speculators were feeling the pinch when real estate was down only 20 percent. With real estate down 50 percent (and more in most metropolitan areas) the majority of speculators will already have been forced to sell or will be in the process of being foreclosed. Most speculators will not sell soon enough to prevent bankruptcy, and the only ones who will survive will be those who have considerable assets unrelated to real estate or those who are only moderately leveraged. Many large speculators who owned 25 houses or more with high leverage will have gone from wealth to bankruptcy unless they had managed to sell out before the crash became widely recognized.

Unfortunately, even homeowners with no speculative intent who purchased homes in the final years of the boom will be experiencing great difficulties. The class of homeowners who put 10 percent to 20 percent down will be looking at huge paper losses should they sell their homes. Only a short time before, these people were viewing their homes as a cash nest egg from which they could siphon money anytime. Many may have hoped to trade up to more expensive homes. Now they will somehow have to make their payments or they will lose their house and be in debt besides. Many of these folks will be forced to sell, and others will sell in an attempt to prevent further losses as real estate continues to drop.

The second class of homeowners, those who purchased early in the boom, put a large amount down, or have substantial non-real-estate-related assets will be the only relatively stable group of homeowners. They will not be *forced* to sell. However, some may opt to sell to prevent further loss of capital. Even those who do not opt to sell will not likely be interested in acquiring more expensive homes at this juncture.

Both of these large groups of homeowners, who suffered scarcely any problems or even worry when real estate was down

133

20 percent, will now be feeling the full effects of the real estate crash. They will be scrambling to keep their heads above water just as the speculators were doing somewhat earlier.

Financial institutions will be greatly affected by the real estate crash. Banks, for instance, loan money that is backed by assets that are significantly related to real estate. Savings and loan institutions and mortgage loan companies have assets that are almost entirely made up of real estate. Obviously, a drop in real estate values will represent a sharp loss of assets for these companies and institutions. Additionally, the financial crunch that forces speculators, and now other homeowners, into ruin will leave lending institutions with bad debts and foreclosures; their real estate loans will suddenly be turning into just plain real estate, and much less valuable real estate at that.

Under the crunch of a devalued portfolio of assets and unusually high levels of loan default, the management practices of many financial institutions will be under harsh scrutiny. They will have to weather some very stormy days. Many who have committed themselves too far will have inadequate security remaining to handle the loan losses they will sustain. Many will fail. What will be important to the financial community and to the entire economy will be the rate of failure.

Once people begin to realize the tenuous situation of banks and savings and loans, deposits will begin to flow from these once-safe havens. Savings are theoretically insured up to $40,000 by the FDIC and the FSLIC, but these insurance corporations hold available only one percent to 2 percent of the amount of money they are pledged to insure. Any large-scale collapse of banks or savings and loan companies, even if only a small fraction of the total of such institutions, could put a heavy strain on the limited insurance assets. Even worse, an unusual number of institutional failures (again even if only a small percentage of the total number of such institutions) could shake public confidence in the safety of savings accounts. Though this shaken confidence may not produce a 1930s-style run on the banks, every dollar taken out of a savings account by an anxious depositor will result in a further diminishment of money behind institutional assets at a time when institutions will need all the money they can get.

CONFIDENTIAL BULLETIN

THIS IS A SECOND DEED OF TRUST
File No. ___Y15502-MP___

LOAN TERMS

AMOUNT $15,000.00   TERM __36__ mos.
INTEREST RATE 10%
MONTHLY RETURN 125.00   INTEREST
PREPAYMENT BONUS TO INVESTOR: Upon voluntary prepayment, six (6) months interest on eighty percent (80%) of the unpaid balance, or interest to maturity, whichever is lesser.
BALANCE DUE AT MATURITY $ 15,000.00

HOUSE AND PROPERTY
Approx. sq. ft. House __1200__ Garage __400__ Lot __50x125__
Layout __LR,DR,KIT,3BR, 1-1/2BA, FENCE__
__COV. PATIO, SPRINKLER SYSTEM__

Address of Property __1106 James Avenue, Redwood City__

EQUITY ANALYSIS
Appraiser's estimate of current market value . . . . $ 55,000.00
Present balance of 1st deed of trust . . $ 24,675.00
Held by __Peterson Mortgage Co.__
Monthly Payment __247.50__ Int. __8%__
Original amount of 1st was $ __26,825.__
Impounds Included __yes__ Term __30__ Yrs.
Origination date __Dec. 1968__

PROTECTIVE EQUITY $ __30,325.00__
Amount of your loan . . . . $ __15,000.00__

BORROWERS
Position __Electrician__
Firm __Smith Electric Company__
How long __6 yrs.__ Annual income $22,500.
Position __Housewife__
Firm ____
How long ____ Annual income ____

PURPOSE: __consolidation__
COMMENTS: __Good demand in area. Well-maintained. Close to conveniences.__

As hard as the crash in real estate values will be for banks and savings and loans, they will look strong indeed in comparison with mortgage loan companies that specialize in second mortgages.* Second mortgages are made to release some of the accumulated equity in originally mortgaged homes. Since second mortgages are subject to the rights of first-mortgage holders they are much more risky loans. Still, despite the risk and despite the financial catastrophe suffered by second-mortgage holders earlier in this century, mortgage loan companies are a huge and thriving business heavily advertising their 10 percent plus returns. One California company, by no means the largest, boasted of making more than $34 million in loans in 1977. This loan volume was supported by investors who hope to receive

---

* Second mortgages are now called second deeds of trust or first second deeds of trust by this industry that is eager to avoid the stigma attached to the words "second mortgages," particularly in the minds of folks who remember the years from 1925 to 1940 when huge sums of money were lost by second-mortgage holders.

a return on their money that in some states ran higher than 10 percent. Many retired people we know have invested substantial sums of money with these companies. But with the fallout of real estate prices, these institutions will fail by the thousands. Having to pick over whatever money is left in the event of foreclosure and bankruptcy, second-mortgage holders will feel the same shock felt by other financial institutions, only amplified manyfold.

Finally, we have one of the largest groups of them all, the home builders. Each time the financial institutions described above sneeze, the home building industry catches cold—the industry is so dependent on the availability of money and credit. In recent years, with demand at record highs and with developers literally forced to hold lotteries in order to determine who could buy a home, home builders have been a good lending risk and have not had to work very hard to get enough capital to build. Even when zoning and environmental restrictions lengthened the lead-time necessary to complete a project, the money continued to flow.

During the crash, however, home builders will not only find a greatly reduced demand for their current inventories, they will also find a money supply that has dwindled to a trickle or stopped as banks, savings and loans, and mortgage institutions fight to keep themselves above water.

The home builders, whose business has typically been feast or famine, will be embarking on their greatest famine ever—perhaps worse than in the 1930s. Builders will now own huge inventories of unsold houses, declining in value each day. Those with large inventories will be in the same situation as the REITS a few years ago. The banks will become nervous about the loans made to builders and will be threatening to put them into bankruptcy. A substantial number of construction workers in the housing-related segment will be out of work.

18

The Aftermath

As the crash deepens, full public awareness will develop. At first only speculators, large real estate investors, home builders, and lending institutions will be hurt. But soon homeowners will become very aware that they have lost a lot of equity; they will have lost buying power. Homeowners will have to tighten their belts as the "savings accounts" once represented by their homes are destroyed. Consumer spending will dry up, and all segments of the economy will feel the shockwave generated by the real estate avalanche. Public attention will shift to preventing the shock wave from engulfing the entire economy. Thus, the government will step in—the representative of the public.

You may be wondering why we have not discussed the government before now. We have often been confronted with the view that the government could not allow real estate to crash—it would destroy our economy. The government, however, will not realize the severity of the real estate decline any sooner than the public.

Just as in past economic upheavals, governmental and public action will likely occur after the fact. Not until 1933 and 1934, long after the stock market crash, were security laws passed aimed at preventing the excesses that had occurred several years earlier. A more modern example would be the governmental action over the energy crisis. For years prior to 1973 our dependency on foreign oil was mushrooming. The energy crisis was predicted years earlier, but the government and the public ignored these predictions. In October 1973 public awareness finally materialized, thanks to the Arab oil embargo. Not only was the government unable to formulate an energy policy then, but five years later it has still not been able to do much. Meanwhile, oil became plentiful, but due to the marketplace's upward adjustment in oil prices rather than to governmental action.

The government will enter the picture during the aftermath of the real estate crash. Even without action for some time, the normal preliminary rhetoric and jawboning will help restore confidence. Simultaneously, the marketplace will be diverting money from real estate to more productive areas. The government will initially concentrate on the segments of the economy most obviously in trouble.

The crash will have caused speculators and homeowners to abandon the market in huge numbers, and lending institutions will have sharply stiffened their lending requirements to protect their suddenly diminished total assets. These assets will be threatened all the more as hard-pressed homeowners withdraw savings to try to balance their own budgets. If a substantial number of financial institutions fail, other depositors will remove money from the remaining institutions to invest in "disaster hedges" like gold, silver, and high quality bonds. With this gloomy picture unfolding across the country, the first segment government will help will be the banks and savings and loan companies.

Though the primary problem suffered by banks and savings and loans will come from their devalued real estate assets, the state of their balance sheets will not constitute their immediate crisis. This is because large lending institutions often use creative accounting procedures. Real estate losses can be disguised to an extent as long as an adequate volume of routine deposits is maintained. But a loss of faith on the part of current and potential depositors would expose the paper millions on the balance sheets and result in a dangerous, if not fatal, shortage of liquid assets to pay off the doubters who come to the counter for their cash.

To head off panic runs by depositors, banks and savings and loan companies will begin to stress in their advertising the safety of their "insured deposits." Yet, as we have pointed out, the FDIC and the FSLIC have only a very small proportion of the funds they would need to meet a crisis of confidence. Further, neither of these insurance corporations has ever been put to the test. There have been several massive failures of financial institutions in the recent past, but in each instance, the bankrupt or insolvent institution has been absorbed by larger and stronger institutions that have, in turn, honored the deposits.

At a time, however, when nearly every bank is suffering a sharp decline in the value of its assets, such an institutional takeover will be much more risky, so the federal government will bolster its deposit insurance corporations so that the public will be convinced of the safety of its savings. The level of money then available to the FDIC and FSLIC, despite urgent rhetoric from Washington, will be insufficient to restore public confidence. To guarantee confidence, Congress will have to increase the funds available for deposit insurance. This will probably be done through emergency legislation that would allow insurance corporations to dip into general tax revenues if needed. The time period in which deposit insurance payments would be received will have to be specified, and there will undoubtedly be a great deal of jawboning by the government to keep corporate deposits in American banks rather than having them go to safer institutions outside the country.

Though at a tremendous cost to taxpayers, these measures,

139

if taken quickly enough, will likely avert complete economic. collapse. But the government will not be out of the picture immediately, for the next group of complaining voices that will find an ear in Washington will be the millions of homeowners who will be faced with the prospect of losing their homes. To help this desperate and politically powerful group, Congress will pass some form of mortgage assistance, particularly for those who have been thrown out of work by the economic crisis. It is possible that the law may be amended to allow homeowners to deduct the losses they suffered on their homes when sold.* Meanwhile, state and local governments will be under merciless pressure to reduce property taxes. There may be ways to refinance loans for homeowners who find the value of their homes lying below the amount of their outstanding mortgage. Since the government already finances nearly 55 percent of all home mortgages in the nation today, it would be in a position to plan and enact such refinancing schemes.

No matter which of these or other strategies the government employs, it will be under sizzling political pressure to do something—quickly. Home builders, for instance, will need governmental assistance desperately. The nation's sprawling home construction industry, its workers, developers, contractors, and suppliers will be awash in red ink. Nearly everyone in the building trades industry will be unemployed. The inventory of unsold homes and homes under construction will be staggering in the face of the reduced demand that will result from diminished investment incentives, high down payments, and stricter lending requirements.

Faced with a desperate building trades industry, the government will undoubtedly try to legislate incentives for home building and buying. These may include making large tax credits available to those who purchase houses to live in themselves. To overcome the problems of high down payments and restrictive lending requirements the government may guarantee and subsidize mortgages.

Although this is not an exhaustive list of possible government responses to the housing crisis, they and others will stand a good chance of restoring confidence in the market so that the

* The law currently stipulates you cannot write off a loss taken on your home.

economy will not collapse completely. But real estate prices will stabilize at much lower levels than have been seen in decades. Moreover, the federal government will be regulating real estate. This regulation will be aimed at preventing another boom. However, even without government regulation there will not be another boom in real estate until a new generation matures, untouched by this crash.

Part Five

How to Profit and Protect Yourself

19

The Average
Homeowner and You

As our real estate boom has gathered speed over the last few
years, the proportion of people's total worth that is represented
by real estate has increased dramatically. A house that was once
no more than a place to live and raise a family became a store-
house of cash as second mortgages or refinancing were available to homeowners to tap the rapidly increasing equity.

According to figures compiled by a large savings and loan
company, the average homeowner in 1978 owned a house
worth $50,000, a mortgage loan with $15,000 still outstanding,
and other assets totalling $32,500. These assets included sav-

ings, insurance cash values, and other investments, as well as such personal property as automobiles, appliances, and furniture. Our average homeowner owes an installment debt of $8,500 on these possessions.

Based on these figures, the average homeowner's balance sheet looks like this:

Assets		Liabilities	Net Assets
House	$50,000	$15,000	$35,000
Savings and investment (not real estate)	12,500	none	12,500
Personal property	20,000	8,500	11,500
Totals	$82,500	$23,500	$59,000

Thus, average homeowners find 60 percent of their assets and 85 percent of their net worth in their homes.

As healthy as this balance sheet appears, the concentrations of money in one investment outlet is a sign of vulnerability under the best of circumstances. At this point in the real estate market, a high concentration of real-estate-related investments is dangerous indeed. When the decline in real estate values begins, an average family will watch its total worth decline. If the money an average homeowner has invested outside his home is in another house or real-estate-related investments, the degree of vulnerability increases still further.

To simplify this examination, let's assume that our average homeowners, who we'll call the Joneses, do not have investments in any real estate other than their home. What will happen to them when the crash comes?

In many parts of California, Colorado, Illinois, and in Washington, D.C., prices have been lashed by extraordinary levels of speculation. In Orange County, California, for example, the land rush has been so spirited that prices of existing homes have more than tripled since 1970. As speculators in these areas are forced to abandon the market, prices could easily drop to one-half to one-third of their current levels. Other parts of the country, where speculation is not so widespread, may be more fortunate.* To be conservative, we will place the Jones family in a suburb of a large metropolitan area where extreme levels of speculation did not occur, and assume the eventual drop in the value of their home will be only one-third.

With a one-third decline in housing prices, the Jones family will find that the value of their $50,000 house will dip to $33,000. Their balance sheet will now look like this:

Assets		Liabilities	Net Assets
House	$33,000	$15,000	$18,000
Savings and Investment (not real estate)	12,500	none	12,500
Personal property	20,000	8,500	11,500
Totals	$65,500	$23,500	$42,000

To put a time perspective into our example, let's assume that it will take prices three years to bottom after their peak. In those years the Joneses will find that they have lost $17,000, or 29 percent of their net worth. If we add the fact that in those three years there will be none of the growth the Joneses had been anticipating, they will, in fact, have only about half the amount of money they had been expecting.† The significance of this decline in real assets against expectations will be sharply felt by the Joneses if they, like many homeowners, had planned to use the anticipated equity to finance their children's education or their own retirement. Rather than providing a fund of cash for these future plans, our average family now finds itself with worries about meeting their monthly payments.

* Though undoubtedly there will be a few locations across the country that will remain unaffected by the turndown in prices because of special situations, homeowners should be careful to avoid the trap of thinking that their particular area will be exempt. This same reasoning was used by boomtime investors in all of the historical booms we've studied, and it was this thinking that led to ruin.
† The Joneses, like nearly everyone else, probably expected their house to increase in value by 10 percent a year. In three years its value would be $67,000, increasing their net worth to $76,000, versus the less attractive $42,000 shown on the above chart.

147

Can the Jones family, and the thousands of homeowners like them, do anything to prevent economic misfortune? The answer is clearly yes. But to prevent a decline in their net worth, the Joneses, and homeowners like them, will have to realize that the declining value of their homes represents a *real* loss of money. This fact may not be as clear to most homeowners as it appears. Many bought their homes 10 to 15 years ago at relatively modest prices, and these homeowners may feel that their original investment is all that they are risking. This mental attitude is as curious as it is pervasive. Had, for instance, the Joneses put $20,000 into time bank deposits 15 years ago and averaged a 6 percent annual rate of interest, the original $20,000 would now be worth $50,000.

If, because of a bank failure, the Joneses were to lose a third of this accumulated capital, $17,000, they would be quite upset. The Joneses must realize that the loss of equity they will suffer in the real estate devaluation will be a loss of exactly the same dollars; money that could be used to pay medical expenses, send a child to college, or buy a new camper. The fact is that dollars in their home's equity are the same dollars as those in the bank. Moreover, were they now to take $50,000 and put it into safe government bonds, which are, at this writing, earning 8½ percent interest, they would find that in three more years they would have $64,000, adding $14,000 to their net worth as opposed to a $17,000 loss—a difference of $31,000!

Given these figures, it is obvious that the best course for the Joneses and homeowners like them would be to sell their homes and reinvest the proceeds in an acceptable alternative investment. If they were to follow this course, the Joneses would receive $35,000 from their home, less any transaction costs. They would also have to pay the long-term capital gains on the profits they receive unless they repurchase a home or begin construction on a new home within 18 months from the sale. If they did not repurchase within the alloted time the tax would amount to 40 percent of the current tax rate, and through the use of income tax averaging this figure could be distributed over the last five years. In all probability the tax bite would be only from 10 percent to 15 percent of their profits. This would amount to approximately $3,000 for the Joneses. So they would realize a total of $32,000 that they could invest in government bonds at 8½ percent interest. The interest would provide them $2,720 a year, or $227 a month. No longer having to pay mortgage installments, property taxes, insurance, or repairs, the Joneses would find that it would be cheaper for them to rent a comparable house than to own their own home.

If the Joneses are reluctant to move, they might try a strategy that has been successful for many families. Since there are currently many speculators who are still trying to buy houses for appreciation, it is often possible to find a buyer for a house who will allow the former homeowner to continue living in the house as a long-term renter. This strategy allows a family to stay in its home while transferring the risk of price decline to the speculator.

But will the Joneses, and others like them, be willing to become renters? Most homeowners have worked hard to become and remain homeowners, particularly with soaring costs the last few years. Would the money saved by renting be worth giving up home ownership? The reason the Joneses should sell their home and invest in an acceptable alternative investment is not simply to make money, but to assure themselves of being able to be homeowners after the crash. Eighty-five percent of their net worth is in a risky investment—risky only because the boom has caused dramatic investment and speculative excesses to be applied to their dwelling. It would be nice if a home were still just a home; then the Joneses would have no reason to sell. But such is not the case.

Perhaps a more rewarding reason for the Joneses to sell is so they can soon purchase their "dream house." This apparent fancy can become reality if the Joneses are able to select a good alternative investment that will produce income plus appreciation in value. They can be doubling their money as real estate values are slashed to one-half or one-third of their previous highs. This occurrence would mean that in the depths of the crash the Joneses could draw on their accumulated cash to buy a house worth many times as much as the one they sold earlier. They will have their pick of homes, as most homeowners will have lost vast sums of money and the Jones family will be one of the "lucky" ones who can buy at this time. The Joneses may even be able to find a bargain within the 18-month period and escape the $3,000 they might have paid in tax on the sale of their home. Having sold their home and being willing to rent for a while, the Joneses will have the utmost flexibility, while others are scrambling to hold onto their homes or, more likely, being foreclosed against and scrambling to hold off bankruptcy.

Despite the wisdom of selling property now, in advance of price declines, the Joneses may, like many homeowners, not be willing to become renters even for a while, or may feel this is too much trouble. If so, they will likely not profit from the devaluation of real estate. Nevertheless, it will be imperative that they protect themselves against the forced sale of the home they want to keep.

The Joneses' original balance sheet showed 60 percent of their total assets and their total equity was in their home.

Assets		% of Total	Liabilities	Equity	% of Total
House	$50,000	60%	$15,000	$35,000	60%
Savings & Investments (not real estate)	12,500	15%	none	12,500	21%
Personal property	20,000	25%	8,500	11,500	19%
Total	$82,500		$23,500	$59,000	

Value of house is 85 percent of net worth.

By using second mortgages or refinancing, they would probably be able to pull at least $25,000 out of their accumulated equity, and could reinvest it. If the Jones family were to take this strategy their balance sheet would look like this:

Assets		% of Total	Liabilities	Equity	% of Total
House	$ 50,000	47%	$40,000	$10,000	17%
Savings & Investments (not real estate)	37,500	35%	none	37,500	64%
Personal property	20,000	18%	8,500	11,500	19%
Total	$107,500		$48,500	$59,000	

Value of house is still 85 percent of net worth.

Their net worth has not increased, of course, but the percentage of their total equity that is involved in real estate has dropped from 60 percent to 17 percent. Outside investments not related to real estate now account for 35 percent of their total assets and 64 percent of their equity. In the event of a 33 percent devaluation of the selling price of their home, the Joneses will still lose $17,000 in total assets (perhaps offset by gains in their other investments), but the liquid assets in other investments can be used in case of emergencies that might otherwise have threatened the Jones' ability to meet their mortgage payments. There may not be much of a profit in this strategy, but the Joneses will find that their home is much better protected.

The case of the Jones family is a dramatization of a statistically average American homeowner. From their example, it is clear that the higher the percentage of total assets homeowners have tied to real estate, the greater their vulnerability. To see how you compare with the Joneses, fill in the tables below.

I. To find total real estate assets, liabilities, and equity

ASSETS		LIABILITIES	
Home	————	Real Estate Mortgages	————
Other Real Estate	————		————
Second Mortgages owned	————		————
First Mortgages owned	————	Real Estate Taxes	————
Other Real-Estate-Related Investments	————	Other Real Estate Liabilities	————
A. Total Assets	————	B. Total Liabilities	————
C. Total Equity (A − B)	————		

II. To find total assets and total equity you have in non-real-estate savings and investments

ASSETS		LIABILITIES	
Cash	_____	Loans against any	_____
Savings Accounts	_____	Savings or Investment in this area	_____
Checking Accounts	_____	Potential Tax Liability	_____
Stocks	_____	Federal	_____
Bonds	_____	State	_____
		Local	_____
Insurance Policy Cash Values	_____	Other Liabilities Related to this Area	_____
Deferred Annuities	_____		
Keogh Plan	_____		
IRA Plan	_____		
Profit-Sharing Vested Now	_____		
Retirement Plan Vested Now	_____		
Accounts Receivable	_____	E. Total Liabilities	_____
Other Liquid Savings or Investment Assets	_____		
D. Total Assets	_____		
F. Total Equity (D − E)	_____		

III. To find the value of your personal property

This part can be tricky since it is hard to know for what price you could actually sell your possessions. Be conservative, assuming you had to sell everything in a very short period of time.

ASSETS		LIABILITIES	
Automobiles (Blue Book Values)	————	Charge Cards	————
Other Motor Vehicles	————		————
Furniture	————		————
Silver and China	————		————
Art and Heirlooms	————	Installment Loans	————
Home Appliances (not attached to house)	————	Automobile Loans	————
Equity in Business	————	Other Loans or Debts	————
Other Personal Property (not clothes)	————		
G. Total Assets	————	H. Total Liabilities	————
I. Total Equity (G – H)	————		

ASSETS	% Of Total Assets	Liabilities	Equity	% Of Total Equity
A. Real Estate	A/J	B. ____	C. ____	C/L
D. Savings and Investments (not real es- tate)	D/J	E. ____	F. ____	F/L
G. Personal Prop- erty	G/J	H. ____	I. ____	I/L
Totals J. ____		K. ____	L. ____	(Net Worth)

Percentage of Net Worth in Real Estate   A/L _____

To find out the percentage of your total assets that you have in real estate, in savings and investments other than real estate, and in personal property, divide figure A by J, D by J, and G by J, respectively. To find the percentage of total equity that you have in each area divide C by L, F by L, and I by L respectively. To find the percentage of your net worth that you have in real estate divide A by L.

To determine your level of vulnerability to a drop in real estate values, it is most important to note the percentage of your total assets in real estate compared to the percentage in savings and in other forms of outside investment. Next in importance is the percentage of your equity that is real estate related. Of least importance to most people is the percentage of net worth made up by real estate, though if you have unusually high real estate assets, the importance of this figure increases. If, for instance, you have assets of $120,000 in real estate and a net worth of $60,000, a 50 percent decline in real estate values will, for you, mean insolvency.

Whatever your situation, you should quickly attempt to lower the percentage of your assets and equity represented by real estate. If you own real estate other than your own home, we strongly recommend that you sell it expeditiously.

If you own second mortgages, it is imperative that you get out of them. First mortgages should be all right, providing the real estate is currently worth at least three times the outstanding mortgage loan.

To be in a position to profit fully from the coming devaluation of real estate, it will be necessary to transfer all of your assets out of real estate and real-estate-related investments. But if you must hang on to your house, with each investment diversification you will find yourself in a better position.

In short, your figures should show that you are, at the very least, keeping up with the Joneses. Otherwise, unless you are in much better shape than the average homeowner, you will stand to lose considerably over the next few years.

20

Alternative Investments

In this chapter we will be discussing alternative investments to real estate. It is important to realize there are other major capital markets from which to choose and that all investments compete with each other for investment dollars. As you will soon see, there are distinct periods when one of these investments is clearly a better value than the others and, consequently, a more profitable place to have your money.

For more than a decade, the best capital market to be in has been real estate. This has not always been the case; and for the reasons we have presented thus far, real estate is again about to lose its status as the best investment. The real estate market is in a deadly boom cycle, and the inevitable crash may be hastened by the realization that the fundamentals behind the boom are attenuating. We can also see from a pure investment standpoint, too, that real estate is simply overvalued.

Ten years ago, an investor who bought a house or apartment building for 20 percent down could expect to receive a 10 to 20 percent return. This is called a positive cash flow. Today, however, expenses such as taxes and financing have virtually eliminated the possibility of a positive cash flow at current purchase prices. In California, for example, it is not unusual to find people of average means buying $100,000 houses at 10 percent down, who then are forced to rent them for less than $500 a month. These people are *losing* at least $400 to $500 a month, after paying insurance, taxes, maintenance, and mortgage payments. The rationale behind such "investments" is that the expenses are tax-deductible and price increases are more than making up for the monthly losses. But tax losses are easy to find in many other areas, and if healthy price increases are necessary simply to break even, such a purchase is hardly an investment—it is a speculation. Investments provide safety and income, and while it is desirable to obtain growth, it is not paramount to survival.

It has been argued that, although a negative cash flow does exist today, rental income will grow and ultimately will be sufficient to provide an income. In many areas, however, even under the most optimistic circumstances, this process would take a very long time. If rental income increased at a healthy 7 percent annually, for example, it would still take more than 10 years to double (the increase needed for a positive cash flow in most metropolitan areas).

Beyond the fact that the residential market is overvalued in its historical worth as an investment, it is also overvalued in terms of other investments. Consider the financial sense of buying a house at today's high prices versus renting a comparable house and taking the cash to other investment markets where conservative investments are bringing an annual return of more than 8½ percent.

A new homeowner paying cash for a $60,000 house will have the added expense of some $1,200 in insurance and taxes each year. (We will ignore the labor and expense of maintenance, although for most homeowners this is considerable.) If, on the other hand, our new homeowner had decided to rent and invest his $60,000 safely at 8½ percent, the resultant annual income would be $5,100. Moreover, the $1,200 in taxes and insurance would be avoided. Adding this $1,200 savings to the $5,100 that the investment would return, provides a total of $6,300, or $525 a month. This amount would currently be more than adequate to rent a comparable home.

For folks using mortgages, the situation is similar. An investor putting 10 percent down on a $60,000 house has invested only $6,000. This would, if otherwise invested, bring only $500 a year. However, the homeowner will be paying $5,400 a year in mortgage payments as well as an approximate $1,200 a year in taxes and insurance, a total outlay of $6,600 a year. The loss of the $500 income from the down-payment of $6,000 raises the real cost of buying the house to a total of $7,100, which represents a monthly cost of $592—much more than would be necessary to rent comparable housing.

It is often argued that a house is preferable to other investments because "you can't live in other investments." As we have seen, however, when real estate prices are high relative to other investments, the income from other investments can provide the funds to rent a comparable place to live. Currently, these alternative investments leave considerable extra income besides. The plain fact is that the cost of owning a house today is quite high while its return is quite low.

Of course, many homeowners point to intangible benefits of ownership. But in the face of what may prove to be the most devastating crash in American history, these benefits will be expensive indeed!

Many folks seem to think that since a large portion of the equity in their home is profit, it is not real money, and thus it will not really make any difference if the price of their home declines. It's like a lucky Las Vegas gambler who has won $100 on the first bet, who figures to gamble with the "house's" money and feels it won't matter if he loses it. The fact is, the gambler could cash in his chips for a $100 bill, a bill that would look no different from one he has worked for.

It is of crucial importance that homeowners realize that the

157

money in their houses is not "play money." It is money that can pay your rent, put food on your table, provide income for retirement. It is money that can pay for entertainment, vacations, and, in many cases, luxuries. It is money that would normally take you many years to save. Most important, it is money that, if invested safely and properly, can provide you with your dream house after the real estate crash is over. Even if you were to sell your house and your capital did not appreciate during the devaluation, you could upgrade your living standards merely because you were one of the few to preserve your purchasing power. Thus, you could start building, or buy your dream house, within 18 months without even having to pay any capital gains tax.

During the real estate crash, mere preservation will be a means of profiting. Our goal in the following pages, however, is not only to preserve your capital once you get it out of the real estate market, but to explain exactly how you can increase it in the years ahead.

HOUSES VERSUS STOCKS

Once the decision is made to remove some or all of your assets from real estate and into non-real-estate-related options, the question is, Which investment should you choose? The two most common types of investment in recent years have been real estate and stocks. But because the stock market has not performed well in recent years, it will probably not be the first option to be explored by investors who have divested themselves of real estate holdings. As most investors form their opinions exclusively from recent history, they assume real estate has performed, and always will perform, better than stocks and thus will not consider the stock market as an alternative.

A long-term examination of real estate investment compared with investment in the stock market, however, reveals some interesting findings.

The graph of stock and house prices shows that in the years between 1890 and 1977, prices for new homes have increased 3 percent annually while stock prices have advanced at a 4.25 percent growth rate, actually outperforming real estate over the long term. Even if we ignore the income from these investments, we must take depreciation into consideration. While the

158

depreciation of a company's assets is reflected in its stock price, the same is not true of houses. As houses decay and depreciate in value we must subtract that depreciation from the median price of a new house to arrive at an accurate comparison between houses and stocks. By depreciating the value of the structure (land does not depreciate) by 2 percent a year, and assuming an average structural life of 50 years, we find that the adjusted price of new houses has grown at an annual rate of 1.7 percent, compared to 4.25 percent for stocks.

Of course, being mortal beings we cannot wait 87 years for an investment to mature. Our graph reveals that the past decade was not the first time real estate soundly outperformed stocks; there have been many distinct periods in the past when this has been the case. So, in order to find an investment strategy suitable to something less than eight decades, we must find which of the two is the better investment today and for the immediate years ahead.

To help us in this determination we will employ a device we call a risk indicator. The risk indicator, which compares houses and stocks as an investment, is derived by taking the annual

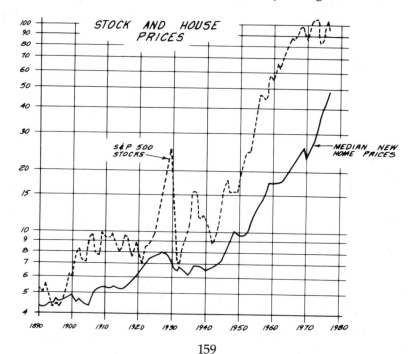

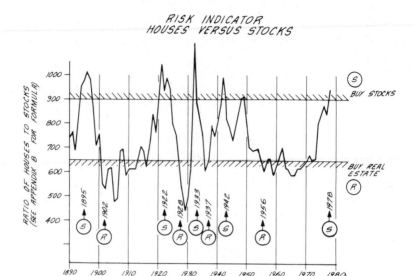

median price of new homes and dividing it by the annual average of the Standard and Poors 500 Stock Index.* When real estate prices are high relative to stocks, our indicator will produce a high number, signaling real estate contains high risk and that stocks are a better value. Conversely, when stock prices are high relative to real estate prices, our indicator will produce a low number, indicating stocks contain high risk and real estate is a better value. We have performed this calculation for each year since 1890 and plotted the result on the above graph. Notice how the indicator constantly moves from one investment to the other, revealing a continuing trade-off between real estate and stocks.

On the graph we have drawn crosshatched, horizontal lines at 650, indicating the area in which stocks contain high risk and real estate is the better value, and at 900, where real estate contains high risk, making stocks a better value.

If individuals using our indicator had alternated between stocks and real estate, selling real estate and buying stocks the year *after* the indicator passed 900 and selling stocks to buy

* See Appendix B.

real estate the year after it dropped below 650, they would have done quite well. Starting in 1895 with stocks, 86 percent would have been made in seven years. A switch to real estate in 1902 offered a 52 percent growth over the next 20 years, at a time when stocks were stagnant. In 1921 the indicator would have signaled a switch to stocks that, if followed in 1922, would have provided a seat on the roaring stock market boom of the 1920s, scoring an increase of 137 percent over six years. The indicator would have signaled a sell of stocks in 1928 that, though perhaps a bit too early, would have avoided the Great Crash of 1929. So it goes. From 1943 to 1956 stocks grew 305 percent, at which point the indicator would have signaled a switch to real estate, which through 1977 would have returned another 250 percent.

Thus investors, had they followed our indicator exactly through the years since 1895, would have earned an average yearly growth rate of 6.72 percent, which compares with 4.25 percent with stocks and 1.7 percent with houses. On the surface this may not seem like an appreciable difference. But using the return generated by our indicator of 6.72 percent, money would double in 10.7 years, as opposed to nearly 17 years for stocks and more than 41 years for houses. If income from rents and dividends are added to this growth figure, the 6.72 percent rate of return would expand to a figure in excess of 12 percent. At that rate, money doubles in six years.

Our indicator, as its name implies, detects relative risk. When stock prices are extremely high relative to real estate prices, history has shown that real estate will outperform stocks and that stocks are extremely vulnerable to a sharp devaluation. The same is true in reverse when real estate prices become extremely high relative to stock prices. At the end of 1977 our risk indicator had reached 941 and was well within the risk zone for real estate. So at the same time that we are seeing a dangerous change in the once optimistic market fundamentals, and an overvalued real estate market that closely parallels previous boom-bust cycles, we also now have further evidence of an imminent devaluation in real estate prices. Clearly, we would be much better off at this point by selling real estate and buying stocks.

161

But, faced with a devastating crash in real estate, with its potential for disruption in the rest of the economy, the risk indicator cannot guarantee stocks will immediately prosper. During crashes in the past, where the entire economy was disrupted, both investments dropped. One simply dropped less than the other. In the great stock market crash of 1929, and during the depression that followed, stocks plummeted severely since this was the investment that contained high risk. But because of the resultant damage to the rest of the economy, real estate also dropped, though at a lesser rate.

In the years ahead, we may face a similar situation. Since most investors hope for more than a strategy for simply losing *less* money, we must compare stocks to a second alternative, which in times of economic upheaval has performed quite well. That other alternative is bonds.

STOCKS VERSUS BONDS

The bond market is a huge capital market that dwarfs both the stock market and the real estate market. Its value is measured in trillions of dollars. We will be looking at the highest-quality bonds.

High-quality bonds are usually thought to be conservative investments. They offer steady income over a span of time that can be as short as days or as long as 40 years; most can be readily sold and are, thus, very liquid assets; and since the initial investment is guaranteed by the issuer, they are quite safe. If you were to buy a $1,000 bond with an 8.5 percent stated yield on face value that matures in 20 years, you could be sure of receiving $85 each year you hold the bond and a full $1,000 back at maturity. From these facts it appears that there is no risk at all attached to a bond purchase short of default by the issuer, a remote possibility indeed for most high-quality bonds.

But there is a risk potential in bond ownership and a profit potential as well. The possibility of both risk and profit is due to the bond's liquidity, for though a bond's face value is guaranteed *at its maturity*, it can be bought and sold before it matures, and its value will fluctuate with the forces of supply and demand. With a face value of $1,000 and a yearly yield of $85, the bond described above was originally sold when yields on high quality bonds were 8.5 percent. But yields change and fluctuate. If today there are fewer investors trying to buy bonds (relative to supply) than there were when our $1,000 bond was purchased, yields on bonds will have increased. Conversely, if more investors have entered the bond market, yields will have declined as the demand increased. These market increases and decreases in yield will have a continuous effect on the market value of your bond. For example, if yields on the high-quality bonds were to increase to 9 percent one year after you bought your bond, it would bring only $949 on the open market. Remember that your bond will always pay $85 each year, so to achieve a 9 percent return on the investment, a buyer would have to require a selling price that was lower than face value. If you were forced to sell your bond under these conditions you would have to absorb a capital loss of $51, or 5.1 percent. This is the risk potential in buying bonds. If, on the other hand, one year after buying the bond from you, the buyer found that the yield on the market had returned to 8.5 percent, a sale of the bond would bring the face value of $1,000 and the buyer of your bond would have in one year made a profit of $51, or 5.37 percent. You'll observe that in the bond market, *profit lies in declining yields and risk in advancing yields.* Thus bond market strategy is the same as stock market strategy. One tries to enter the market when demand is low in order to profit from increasing demand and demand's effect on prices. In the case of our bond example, the effect on prices of a decline in bond yields is quite dramatic.

The Level of Bond Yields	Bond Price	% Increase From the $1,000 Level (or par)
9½%	$ 901	− 10%
9 %	$ 949	−5.1%
8½%	$ 1,000	0%
8 %	$ 1,054	+ 5.4%
7½%	$ 1,112	+11.2%
7 %	$ 1,171	+17.1%
6½%	$ 1,235	+23.5%
6 %	$ 1,302	+30.2%
5½%	$ 1,372	+37.2%
5 %	$ 1,451	+45.1%

Since buying quality bonds with high yields reduces risk in the same way as buying stocks with high secure dividends, the best single indicator for judging the relative value of stocks and bonds is an examination of their respective yields. We have plotted the yields of stocks and bonds over the last 100 years. The dotted line on the graph represents the yields of the Standard and Poors 500 stocks.

The graph shows that between the 1870s and the 1950s stock yields fluctuated between 4 percent and 7 percent. Beginning in the late 1950s, however, rapidly increasing stock prices are indicated by yields that dropped far below their traditional trading range. Yields remain low while stock prices are high, but as the bullish '60s stock market began to cool and the prices began to decline, yields began to increase.

Now look at the other line on the graph. This solid line represents high-quality long-term yields as calculated by Moody's AAA Bond Average. By tracing the progress of the two lines together, you can see that there is a reasonably high differential between stock and bond yields in 1871. From the mid-1870s, however, for the next 60 years shown on the graph, bond yields closely paralleled stock yields. The occasional exceptions to this correspondence occurred when the more active stock market

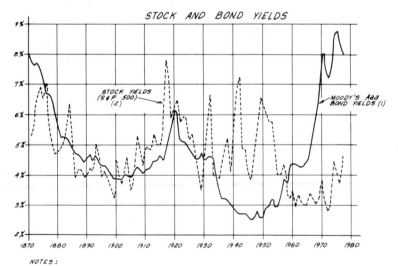

STOCK AND BOND YIELDS

NOTES :
1) INDEX OF AMERICAN RAILROAD BONDS PRIOR TO 1919
2) COWLES INDEX OF common STOCKS PRIOR TO 1937

experienced large short-term changes either up or down. This rough correspondence between stock and bond yields was shattered with the beginning of the Depression. For the next 20 years bond yields dropped and remained far below stock yields. These low bond yields indicate the high prices for bonds caused by heavy investor demand. As the memory of the great stock market and real estate market crashes of the '20s and '30s persisted, investors in large numbers turned to safe, secure, and stable bonds. Bond prices rose and bond yields declined. But in the optimism of the postwar years, investors were less cautious and ventured back into real estate and stocks. The bullish stock market of the '60s and the equally bullish real estate market of the '70s easily attracted much of the available investment capital. In order to compete as an investment, bond yields increased, and our graph shows that yields for bonds soared from 2½ percent in the late '40s, to 8 percent in 1970. As the Housing Boom has continued, so have these extremely high bond yields.

Just as the stock market and the real estate market have historically competed with each other for investment dollars, the bond market has competed with both and has benefited most at times when confidence in stocks and real estate was shaken. At those times of economic uncertainty, the safety and security of bonds made them extremely attractive to investors who were wary of the other markets. At those times bond prices have increased and bond yields declined.*

There is another force that affects bond yields: the inflation rate.

Our next graph shows that bond yields increased during high inflationary periods and decreased during low inflationary and deflationary periods.

There was one exception to this general rule, however: from 1940 through 1947, when the consumer price index increased 75 percent over the period, at a double-digit rate. But bond yields during this period stubbornly remained at 2½ percent to 3 percent. During the uncertainties of World War II, investors

---

* There are occasional periods when stocks and real estate do well and bond yields decline. These periods are aberrations caused by an excessively easy monetary policy in the later 1920s, 1970–73, and 1975. Future aberrations such as this will be in our favor, however, since a decline in bond yields increases bond prices.

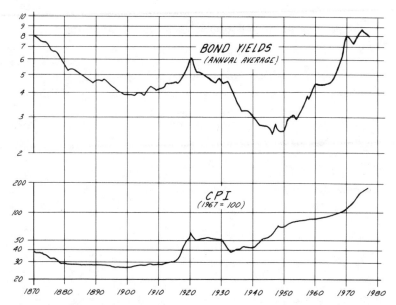

demanded the safety and security that bonds provide even though the inflation rate was increasing.

From history we can see that bond yields will be declining in the years ahead for three basic reasons. The real estate devaluation will certainly cause an economic disruption of some degree, and bonds will represent one of the safest and securest investments. Second, for bonds to compete as an investment vehicle, bond yields have been pushed upward by the outstanding performance of real estate over the last 10 years. But with real estate values dropping, the competition will weaken substantially and bond yields will decline accordingly. Third, a decline in real estate prices will cause a decline in the inflation rate. The consumer price index, the most important indicator of inflation, is influenced heavily by the cost of housing. Nearly 44 percent of the index is determined by home prices, rent, and other housing-related costs.* A decline in home prices will have a depressing effect on both the CPI and the perceived rate of inflation.

The most important fact to be learned from history is that the level of today's bond yields has very few precedents. It is

* Using the new Urban CPI.

166

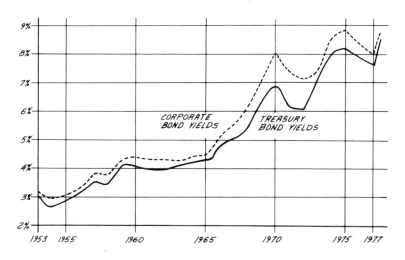

TREASURY AND CORPORATE
BOND YIELDS

CORPORATE
BOND YIELDS

TREASURY
BOND YIELDS

necessary to go back to the Civil War era in this country to find yield levels that rival those in existence at this writing. Bond buyers in those days watched bond yields decline and their bond prices increase for some 40 years.

In this chapter we have dealt with AAA corporate bonds, the highest-quality corporate bonds you can buy. During adverse times when people are looking for safety and security, high-quality bonds will outperform those of lesser grades. There are, however, bonds of even higher quality than AAA corporates, and they are Treasury Bonds issued and backed by the U.S. government. Since Treasury Bonds represent the ultimate in safety, they will yield somewhat less than AAA corporates, but the difference will vary depending on the level of confidence in the economy.

The solid line on the above graph represents yields of 20-year Treasury Bonds.* From 1953 through 1966 the difference between corporate and Treasury Bond yields remained a rather steady ¼ percent. This differential began to widen, however,

* This index has been compiled by the Federal Reserve and only goes back to 1953.

167

as we moved into the 1970s and new economic uncertainties developed. What is important to note, though, is that in the spring of 1978 the differential had narrowed greatly to less than ¼ percent. As the real estate devaluation generates economic problems, not only will bond yields drop, but this differential will widen again, giving Treasury Bonds a superior performance compared to AAA corporates.

Thus, at a time when real estate investments are becoming riskier by the day, Treasury Bonds have, almost literally, never looked so good.

TACTICS

At this writing it is difficult to predict the exact timing and the severity of the coming real estate crash. Thus, it will be necessary for you to find your position in regard to the changing markets at the time you decide to act.

We have divided these tactics into two phases that will correspond to the stages of the real estate crash. Phase One will deal with the market situation that exists today and will continue to exist during those months or years when the crash is under way but not widely perceived. Phase Two will apply once there is widespread public and governmental awareness of declining property prices.

Phase One

There is currently little public awareness of the impending crisis in real estate. The astonishing past performance of real property prices is still widely regarded as a fact of life, and there is little or no perception of risk. Consequently, alternative markets are making lucrative bids for investor attention. Long-term AAA bonds are yielding 8¾ percent, U.S. Treasury Bonds 8½ percent; and while for the most part not competitive with bonds, stock yields are increasing. Standard and Poor's 500 stocks are currently yielding 5 percent.

Compared with the current value of real estate and stocks, bonds are by far the superior investment, with Treasury Bonds more attractive than AAA corporate bonds. A complete list of

Treasury Bonds can be found in many metropolitan newspapers or in the *Wall Street Journal*.* Notations read like this one:

7⅝   2002–07   Feb .... 90.24–91†

This means that the bond has a coupon worth $76.25 (7⅝ percent of par, or $1,000) which will mature in February of 2007. Its asking price is $910. The 2002–07 in the notation indicates that it can be redeemed early (called) in a five-year period between 2002 and 2007. This early redemption feature is of little significance to you, however, since you will be selling the bond long before the dawning of the 21st century.

To further improve your performance using this bond, you can use credit to buy it; the Wall Street term for such credit is *margin*. The procedure is much the same as when loans are used to buy property. Like a mortgage, it involves a down payment, with the remainder borrowed from your broker. A margin loan, though it operates like a mortgage loan, is much less expensive, since there are no prepayment penalties, financing charges, or insurance requirements. Margin loans are simple-interest loans that can run for an indefinite period of time.

The use of margin can be abused. Indeed, margin loans were used extensively and recklessly in the 1920s and did contribute to the losses many people suffered in the Great Crash. But when applied properly to a conservative investment, the use of margin can be quite safe and very lucrative.

One intelligent strategy to use in employing margin is to avoid the maximum permitted amount of leverage. You can buy Treasury Bonds with as little as 10 percent down. But it is usually inadvisable to use such a razor-thin margin. Use of a

* Any Treasury bond quoted with a coupon of 4¼ percent or less is a "flower bond." These bonds are redeemable at face value for estate taxes and thus don't fit into our strategy.

† Treasuries are quoted in whole numbers and usually followed by a decimal point. The number to the right of the decimal point is read in 32nds; 91.17 would be read 91 and 17/32. The price of the bond would be $915.31. The lower of the two numbers is the "bid" and the higher is the "asked" in million-dollar lots. Your cost in smaller amounts could be a few 32nds higher than the asked.

formula of 50 percent down is an intelligent and safe way of employing margin loans to buy Treasury Bonds.

To see how a strategy employing Treasury Bonds and a discreet use of margin can work, let's return to our average home-owning family, the Joneses. You will recall that their house was worth $50,000. Their original balance sheet looked like this:

Assets		Liabilities	Net Assets
House	$50,000	$15,000	$35,000
Savings and Investment (not real estate)	12,500	none	12,500
Personal property	20,000	8,500	11,500
Totals	$82,500	$23,500	$59,000

Were the Joneses to take our advice and sell their house for $50,000, they would have, after subtracting the remainder of their mortgage and capital gains tax, $32,000 in cash. Their balance sheet now looks like this:

Assets		Liabilities	Equity
Savings & Investment (not real estate)	$44,500	none	$44,500
Personal Property	20,000	8,500	11,500
Total	$64,500	$8,500	$56,000

The Joneses are now in a position to easily invest the $32,000 from their house in the high-quality Treasury Bond we described. Using a conservative 50 percent down and a margin loan, they can buy 70 bonds at $910 each for a total investment of $63,700. They will then have invested all of their $32,000 and will have borrowed the remaining $31,700. Assuming a margin-interest rate of 9 percent, and assuming they hold the bonds for three years, they will be charged $7,833 in margin interest (assuming they leave the bond interest in their account).

When, during this three-year period, real estate prices begin to decline, investment activity in the bond market will pick up dramatically and prices will rise while yields will fall. Let's conservatively estimate that bond yields will drop to 6 percent during Phase One of the devaluation cycle. This would mean that each of the Joneses' bonds will increase to $1,226, to a total market value of $85,820. By now the interest income of $16,012 has reduced their margin loan to $23,519. Selling their bonds will leave them with $62,301 after paying back the margin loan, a profit of $30,301 in three years, a gain of 94 percent.

Unfortunately, even if they know their risk, the Jones family, like many other Americans, may not sell their house. This decision will probably eliminate their chances to profit from the real estate crash. But, by refinancing their home and investing the money they free, they can still protect themselves to some extent against loss.

The Joneses should be able to pull $25,000 out of the equity they have in their home through refinancing their first mortgage or taking out a second. This would leave them with $10,000, or 20 percent, equity in their home and a balance sheet that would look like this:

Assets		Liabilities	Equity
House	$ 50,000	$40,000	$10,000
Savings & Investments (not real estate)	37,500	none	37,500
Personal Property	20,000	8,500	11,500
Total	$107,500	$48,500	$59,000

While their net worth has not changed, the Joneses have moved $25,000 into a much safer and more liquid investment.

If they bought their house in the years since 1973, it is likely the Joneses will find that the interest rate on a refinanced first mortgage will be roughly equal to that of their original mortgage. However, if rates on first mortgages are considerably higher than they were when the original mortgage was financed, or if the Joneses find that lending institutions in their area are asking stiff refinancing charges, they may be well advised not to refinance their original loan but to take out a second mortgage instead. Though the interest rate on the second mortgage will be higher, they will, then, have avoided tampering with the low interest rates on the first mortgage and may find that the result is, in fact, cheaper. Most homeowners who

171

are thinking about refinancing their homes will find lending officers willing to advise them on which plan would be less expensive.

For the purposes of this illustration, we'll assume that our average family took $25,000 out of their home equity by using a ten-year second mortgage with an interest rate of 12 percent. This will increase their monthly house payments by $356 for a total over the three years of $12,816. Like most families, the Joneses will not be able to afford this increase in their monthly expenses unless their investment pays at least that well. If they buy the Treasury Bond we used in our former example (7⅝, February 2002–2007, paying $76.25 annually) they would need 56 bonds for the yield to match their increased monthly payments.

These 56 bonds cost $910 each. To purchase them, the Joneses will pay the $25,000 they received from the second mortgage and will borrow the remaining $25,960 on margin from their broker. At 9 percent, this margin loan will cost $8,012 in interest over the three-year period. And when, as in the case of our previous example, the real estate devaluation results in a newly active bond market with yields dropping to 6 percent, the Joneses will find each of their bonds increasing in price to $1,226, a total profit of $9,684. This figure would not likely protect the total loss they would sustain on their home, but the extra cash would allow them more easily to hold on to their home.

To simplify the process of monthly bill paying, the Joneses might ask their broker to send them a check for $356 each month while crediting the semiannual income from the bonds to their account.

If your financial situation is similar to our average family, and if you do not choose to sell your house, you should protect yourself by pulling cash out of it.

Currently, Treasury Bonds are the most profitable conservative investment option, but conditions will change. The following guidelines will help you adjust your investment strategy to changing conditions. The information you will need is available in financial newspapers, libraries and brokerage firms.

Your first step is to go to the risk-indicator formula in appendix B and compute the indicator's value using current an-

nual averages. In the unlikely event the indicator has dropped to 650, you should move back into real estate. However, it is more likely that the indicator will recommend stocks. If stocks are recommended they must be compared to Treasury bonds. To do this you must compare the average annual yield of Standard and Poors 500 stocks with the 20-year Treasury Bond Index, which can be found in most libraries in the monthly *Federal Reserve Bulletin.* If Treasuries are yielding at least 2 percent more than stocks, you should have all of your capital in Treasuries; if Treasuries are less than 2 percent over stocks or even with them, move one-third into stocks; if stocks are yielding up to 2 percent over Treasuries, move two-thirds into stocks; and if stocks are yielding more than 2 percent over Treasuries, you should be fully invested in stocks.

Finally, if this investigation leads you to put all or part of your money in Treasuries, you should check to make sure Treasuries are still a better investment than AAA Corporates. The guideline is simply to keep your money in Treasuries unless AAAs yield more than one percent over Treasuries, in which case you should invest in AAAs.

The diagram above outlines the steps you must take to determine the best place for your money.

Phase Two

Phase Two will begin when the early, subtle stages of the crash have ended and the crash has begun in earnest. At this point the failing real estate market will have attracted widespread public and governmental concern. You, meanwhile, should have made handsome profits with your bonds. As Phase Two dawns, using our guidelines, you will likely begin moving out of bonds and into stocks.

In the depths of the real estate crash, stock prices, reflecting the uncertainty of the economy, will be at relatively low levels. There will be small growth assumptions attached to stocks, and the economic uncertainty should be well anticipated by low prices. Thus, this will be a very safe time to invest in stocks. Just as in Gray's experience with Ford stock during the dark days of the oil embargo, investors will soon realize the future holds a brighter day, and growth assumptions and prices will be on the rise very soon.

Our guidelines for moving from bonds to stocks should be balanced with a word of caution, however. Faced with the most catastrophic crash in American history, it is difficult to predict with confidence the reaction of the federal government. In times of great uncertainty there is, unfortunately, opportunity for great folly. As the economic crisis of Phase Two deepens, there is a small but significant chance that the government will panic and overreact.

To be perfectly safe, you must base the haste with which you sell your bonds upon the prudence of the federal government. We have divided our tactics during Phase Two into two scenarios. Scenario One will deal with an overreaction on the part of government and Scenario Two will deal with the more likely and more reasonable transition.

Scenario One

Overreaction, in this case, would involve a government decision to pump huge amounts of money into the economy to shore up technically bankrupt institutions and individuals. The danger, of course, is that such massive intervention could cause enormous government deficits that would trigger runaway inflation. If this happens, you should act swiftly; for, as the dollar weakens in the face of epidemic inflation, bonds—which are payable in dollars—would be weakened in kind. It would be imperative to sell your bonds even if the stock-and-bond-yield comparison has not already told you to do so, and buy stocks. Stocks perform very well during times of epidemic inflation. The hyperinflated post–World War I German economy is an example.

In making reparations to a vengeful world after World War I, Germany was forced to pay more than its economy could handle and an inflationary spiral developed that quickly reached runaway proportions. During those years Germany became buried in an avalanche of Riechsmarks. Workers were paid daily, and rushed to the grocery store to buy at prices that would often double again the very next day. In 1923 a new currency was finally issued and exchanged for the old inflated Riechsmarks. The exchange rate was one thousand billion of the old marks for one of the new. In the last two years of this hyperinflation stock prices rose six times faster than the inflation rate.

Stocks that will perform best in times of epidemic inflation are those of strong companies with tangible productive assets. These stocks would represent a good value even with an inflation-riddled dollar. You would have partial ownership of the company's tangible assets and, therefore, of its productive capacity—one of the few things of value in such an environment. These companies would include those that own natural resources such as copper, zinc, aluminum, coal, and oil.

In addition to stocks, and only under this scenario, it would be wise to put some of your capital into gold or silver—commodities that hold value well when currency is in trouble. The stocks of the companies that mine those metals would work well also.

Though possible, this scenario is unlikely. After crashes in the past, the government's response has not been to pump up the economy by injecting large amounts of money. The government felt that easy money was, at least partially, the cause of the booms that led to the disasters in the first place, and its typical reaction was to tighten its belt.

In the post–World War I years there was sharp speculation in farm commodities and farm real estate in this country. During 1919 and 1920 the Federal Reserve tolerated the loose credit that financed this boom. But during the crash of 1920–21, the Fed tightened credit conditions, making the resulting depression even worse.

During the Great Crash of 1929, and in the depression that followed, the Fed continued to worry about inflation. Though some 9,000 banks had failed, the memory of Germany's hyperinflation lingered and the Fed tightened. The feeling that easy money had financed the stock market boom was, once again, a major cause of their problems. Andrew Mellon, Hoover's secretary of the treasury said, "Liquidate labor, liquidate stocks, liquidate the farmers. . . ." After that, there would be no way left but up.

Although governmental action is probable, don't overreact. The crash is unlikely to be inflationary. Loosening credit should actually lessen the severity of the crash and soften the blow to the rest of the economy. Only if the outpouring of money is so great that federal deficits increase at rates far above what we have ever seen will inflation reach truly dangerous levels.

Scenario Two

Given the more likely scenario that the government will take a reasonably responsible course of action, we can stick to our original guidelines. In this case we will likely see government intervention in the form of aid to ailing banks and savings and loans and tax breaks for the homeowner and the building industry. We will not, however, see ballooning federal deficits.

There is even a chance that, as in the past, there may be no aid whatsoever. The government may be clamping down on loose money. It may also underestimate the possibility of the crash continuing and therefore feel there is no need for any help. Just as the Great Crash of 1929 was gaining momentum in June 1930, a delegation asked Hoover for a public relief program. His response was, "Gentlemen, you have come sixty days too late. The depression is over." Whether we have responsible aid or no help at all from federal intervention, we will not have a threat of runaway inflation and you can let the stock-and-bond-yield comparison tell you when to move from bonds to stocks.

Stocks that will perform very well in this scenario will be stocks of high quality that offer high yields. Stocks issued by sound utilities, for example, that yield more than bonds are very conservative and should offer growth potential as well as high income. A decline in bond yields will have a very positive effect on utility stocks for two major reasons. First, since both utility stocks and bonds are considered conservative investments and return high income, their yields tend to move in the

176

same direction. A decline in utility yields will mean much higher stock prices. Second, since utilities use bonds to raise capital, bond yields represent a very large cost. Lower bond yields mean utility profits increase and dividends increase. Thus, a decline in bond yields has a double-barreled effect on utility stocks.

In addition, utility dividends usually increase over time (some on a regular annual basis) and offer the potential of growth on their own. Utilities also pay quarterly, as opposed to the semiannual interest from bonds. You can use margin as in the case of bonds, though currently you must put 50 percent down, versus 30 percent for corporates and 10 percent for Treasuries.

Since money will be coming out of the real estate market and into the stock market, most stocks should perform well. Look for good-quality, solid, industrial stocks, at least at first. Your stockbroker spends most of his time with the market and is most qualified to help you with your decision as to which particular stocks to buy. You will be investing in the stock market at a very good time. As long as you diversify somewhat among industries, and stay with good quality, you will do very well.

Initially, your money should go into conservative stocks, like utilities and good-quality industrial stocks. As time passes, as confidence grows, people will invest more aggressively, becoming more growth oriented. Ultimately, the character of the market will change and become more and more speculative, registering quantum leaps on heavy volume. Money will be flooding into the market and margin debt will soar. The public will realize the value it has overlooked for so many years and will stampede into the market just as it did in the late 1920s and the late 1960s. When people get as euphoric about stocks as they currently are about real estate, it will be time to sell. Although this may be a decade or two from now, you should still keep tabs on the risk indicator. When it reaches 650, you should sell your stocks sometime in the following year. Always remember those around you will undoubtedly be consumed with optimism. Do not get caught in the same trap. At that point real estate will be the better investment, and you should take advantage of it again.

OTHER ALTERNATIVE INVESTMENTS

In addition to the capital markets we have already discussed, there are several other alternative investments that offer opportunities to investors who are shifting their money away from real estate.

The most conservative of these investment alternatives is annuities, purchased from insurance companies. An annuity is a contract made with an insurance company to pay a guaranteed income in exchange for a cash deposit. The amount of income depends on the size and type of annuity you buy and on your age. Though an annuity offers no chance of capital appreciation, it does offer substantial income and tax benefits. This may make annuities particularly attractive to older Americans for whom high income and safety are important.

Younger investors may want to explore deferred annuities, which earn interest on a tax-deferred basis. Money invested in deferred annuities currently earns 7–8 percent interest annually. At any time, the deferred annuity can be converted into an immediate annuity or into cash.

A new and interesting use of annuities will become available at some savings and loans in late 1978 or early 1979. It is called a reverse annuity mortgage and may be of particular interest to investors who want to continue to own their own homes. With a reverse annuity mortgage, a savings and loan converts equity in a home—up to 80 or 90 percent of the property's value—into a loan which is, in turn, invested in an annuity. The difference between the monthly annuity payment and the interest on the loan is paid out to the investor each month. There is no obligation to repay the loan unless the property is sold, and the mechanics of the loan and the annuity payments are handled by an insurance company and the savings and loan. Thus a reverse annuity mortgage can result in extra monthly income, with little complication for the homeowner.

Reverse annuities will be of greatest benefit to older homeowners, for whom the income payments can be substantial. However, younger people may elect to purchase a deferred annuity in the same fashion. Often the interest payments can be deducted from tax liability while the annuity is compounding at a tax-deferred rate of 7–8 percent. A purchaser can elect to take the annuity payments at any time, but the longer the annuity remains untapped, the more money will have accumulated. This plus the increasing age of the investor will be factors contributing to higher annuity payments at a later time.

A final relatively conservative investment opportunity is covered stock option writing. This alternative is used in conjunction with a portfolio of common stocks. By writing options on the stocks you own, it is possible to increase your income substantially while covering yourself against market declines. Covered option writing is a bit more risky than annuities but offers a higher reward. Information on option writing can be obtained from most stockbrokers.

So far we have detailed conservative strategies for investing the equity that has accumulated in your home. Since we are recommending that you take your money out of the bloated real estate market to avoid risk, it makes little sense for most investors to increase their exposure in another market.

However, we must point out that the real estate crash will make profound waves in other markets, and instability always opens the possibility of great profits for those investors willing to expose themselves to a much higher risk. The high risk strategies we will briefly describe here require a great deal of attention and timing to succeed. For example, while buying Treasury bonds for cash or with a 50 percent margin loan is a very conservative investment requiring little or no day-to-day attention, putting 10 percent down and borrowing 90 percent (which is currently possible) on the same bond is a very speculative investment. If your timing is good and you correctly anticipate the decline in bond yields, your profits would be enormous. However, a period of adverse fluctuation in the bond market could be enough to require you to come up with more money for margin.

The crash of real estate nationally will have a profound effect on certain areas of the commodity and stock markets. Agile traders will be in a position to profit handsomely. Of particular interest are markets that deal in home-building commodities like lumber and plywood, both of which, no doubt, will decline along with property prices.* If you are familiar with these mar-

* Similarly, purchasing puts or shorting stock of real-estate-related companies will be equally rewarding in the stock market.

kets or can find a professional who is, such high-risk speculation can be quite profitable.

If you have an urge to buy gold and silver as a hedge against the real estate decline, we advise you to resist it. Gold and silver are usually seen as good investments in inflationary times, but when real estate prices fall the inflation rate will also decline. This will result in a diminished market for gold and silver. However, as a hedge against total chaos or monetary collapse, gold and silver still have much merit. (Scenario One).

Similarly diamonds. Though the price of diamonds has risen for each of the last 30 years, there are many problems with them as investments. One problem is that there is an enormous spread between the wholesale and retail price of diamonds. Another is that it takes an expert to determine the price of any single gem, and like gold and silver, diamonds are an inflation hedge and will not do well at a time when the inflation rate is declining.

At this writing, real estate markets are still attracting speculators. As long as this remains the case there is a strategy open to those homeowners who do not wish to sell their homes that may offer partial protection against declining prices. This strategy is the selling of an option on your property. With this strategy, a speculator would pay you immediately for the option to buy your property at a specified price. That is, if you owned a piece of property with a market value of $100,000, you might find a speculator willing to pay you 10 percent, or $10,000, for the option to buy your property at that price at any time during the next 12 months. If prices continue to rise and the option to buy is exercised, you would sell for an effective sales price of $110,000. If, on the other hand, prices begin to fall, you have received $10,000 and can repeat the process at a lower level. In this fashion you can continue to hedge yourself against price declines as long as there are speculators in the market.

One of the most rewarding alternative investments to many will be an investment in themselves. The $25,000, $50,000, $100,000 and more residing in many homes today can be a tremendous tool for a brighter future.

Several people we know have already sold their homes to raise capital for starting their own businesses or other enterprises. The ballooned equities available in their homes provided them with the freedom to try to make it on their own and not have to forever punch a clock for someone else. Although this is a risky investment alternative, many ex-homeowners will be able to reduce the risk by starting with sufficient capital. If you have the initiative, talent and desire to go into business for yourself, it could be your best option out of real estate.

Finally, for those homeowners who plan to adopt none of the strategies we have described and who intend to gamble on the possibility of the inevitable not happening, a word on bankruptcy. In many states the dollar amount of assets exempt from creditors in the event of bankruptcy is surprisingly high. Personal property, cash in federally chartered savings and loans, and the cash value of life insurance are among the categories that are, up to certain levels, exempt. The limits vary from state to state. If, as a result of loss of equity, you should become insolvent, you can move remaining assets into exempt categories before declaring bankruptcy. You can even move to a state where exemptions are higher. If you do nothing else, you should at least formulate a plan for declaring bankruptcy.

21

Real Estate and Other Investments in the Years Ahead

A book has limitations when it comes to giving timely, specific advice to homeowners and investors. It has to be somewhat general, and the lead time before publication and distribution can be prohibitive. We feel this book is enough ahead of events to give most of its readers the information they need to make prudent investment decisions. However, we know conditions can and often do change quite rapidly. Consequently, we will be initiating an advisory letter updating information on real estate and other investments and the condition of the economy as a whole. We will begin publication in the latter half of 1979. If you think you might be interested in seeing our letter, send your name and address to us at P.O. Box 487, Walnut Creek, CA 94596. Other comments or questions you may have can be sent to the same address.

Appendices

APPENDIX A

The 1976 Tax Reform Act

INTEREST AND TAXES
DURING CONSTRUCTION

Perhaps the most significant change in the Tax Reform Act mandates that interest and taxes paid during construction can no longer be treated as current-year expenses. For residential real estate these expenses must now be spread evenly over a period of years that does not begin until after the properties are sold. In 1978, this period is four years. It increases to five years in 1979 and continues to increase to a maximum of 10 years in 1984. The new law began this "phasing in" process on commercial real estate in 1976.

For investors investing in real estate projects these expenses will no longer provide a meaningful initial tax write-off.

INTEREST DEDUCTIONS

Previously, interest expenses incurred on investment were deductible up to the sum of $25,000 plus net investment income and certain other items. Moreover, if the interest expense exceeded this sum, the total deduction could be increased by one-half the excess.

The TRA reduced the maximum interest deduction to $10,000 plus the net investment income. This new restriction directly affects taxpayers currently buying residential income property and houses as investments since these properties generally do not yield a net income before taxes. Now a negative cash flow is deductible only to $10,000 a year.

The treatment of prepaid interest has also changed. Whether on your own home or on other property, prepaid interest can no longer be deducted in the current year that it is paid. The deduction must now be spread over the life of the loan.

The payment of "points" when buying investment property is now treated as prepaid interest and also must be spread over the life of the loan. Although points are still fully deductible in the same year you buy your own residence, they must not be in excess of general business practices in your area.

These new limitations on interest deductions remove another tax advantage and, for many investors, tremendously lower the after-tax return on real estate.

RECAPTURE OF DEPRECIATION

By depreciating real estate at a faster rate than straight-line depreciation, investors can obtain a larger tax write-off during the early years. When the property is sold, however, the depreciation in excess of straight line is "recaptured" and taxed as ordinary income.

Prior to the TRA, there was an escape from this recapture. Once residential property was held longer than 100 months, the excess depreciation subject to recapture was reduced by one percent per additional month it was held. Once investors held the property 200 months there was no recapture whatsoever. This meant investors could obtain large tax write-offs through accelerated depreciation and turn over the property periodically to repeat the process with little or no recapture.

Since 1976, however, this loophole has been plugged. All depreciation in excess of straight line is unconditionally taxed as ordinary income when the property is sold, regardless of the holding period.

TAX PREFERENCE

In addition to plugging the recapture loophole, the write-off through accelerated depreciation is not as generous. The depreciation of real estate in excess of straight-line depreciation is a "tax preference" item.* Prior to the TRA, preference items were exempt from an additional tax up to $30,000 plus the amount of regular income taxes paid on nonpreference items. Any gain in excess of the exemption was subject to an additional tax of 10 percent. For example:

Total tax preference items	$50,000
Less:	
1) Exemption	-$30,000
2) Regular income taxes	-$10,000
Subject to an additional 10% tax of $1,000	$10,000

As you can see the deduction of the exemption and regular income taxes reduced the tax bite tremendously. This allowed accelerated depreciation of real estate to provide investors with large write-offs during the early years of investment without much of an additional tax penalty.

Under the new TRA, however, the exemption is now limited to $10,000 or one-half the regular income taxes, whichever is greater. Furthermore, the additional tax has been increased from 10 percent to 15 percent. Now our example looks like this:

Total tax preference items	$50,000
Less:	
1) Exemption	-$10,000
2) Regular income taxes	-$10,000
Subject to an additional 15% tax of $4,500	$30,000

Under the new law the tax on preference items, such as the depreciation in excess of straight line, has increased greatly—in the above example by 4½ times.

---

* Tax preference items are those income or expense items that have a "preferred" tax treatment.

LIMITED PARTNERSHIPS

A large portion of real estate investment capital is obtained through the formation of "limited partnerships." Under this arrangement many individual investors pool their money to form a partnership and their risk is limited to the amount invested. Previously, initial write-offs could be generated that were in excess of the original investment. This meant the risk was reduced substantially since the tax savings could approach the initial investment. If the investor's tax bracket was high enough, a large write-off was worth more than the property itself.

Write-offs are now much more difficult, and the TRA further stipulates that limited partners can no longer write-off more than they invest, since that is what they have at risk.

With this new restriction, together with the restrictions on obtaining write-offs through interest and depreciation, public real estate limited partnerships have lost much of their tax shelter appeal, and another source of demand has been curtailed.

VACATION HOMES

Further evidence of the trend on real estate taxation is the more restrictive rules regarding expenses incurred on vacation homes.

If you occupy your vacation home for more than 14 days or for more than 10 percent of the days it is rented, the deductions you can take for operational expenses and maintenance cannot exceed the income generated after other deductions, such as interest and taxes. If the house is rented for fewer than 15 days, expenses and income are not tax considerations. In other words, you can no longer use operational and maintenance expenses on your vacation home to shelter other income if one of three conditions exists: if you occupy it for more than 14 days a year, if you occupy it for more than 10 percent of the days it is rented, or if it was rented for fewer than 15 days out of the year.

Appendix B

The Risk Indicator Calculation

In order to find an indicator that fluctuates between 500 and 1,000, we need to compensate for the superior long-term performance of stocks. A factor must be added to the ratio of houses and stocks to keep the indicator fluctuating horizontally as opposed to a downward-sloping path. This factor is calculated by taking the current year, subtracting 1905, and multiplying the result by six. The formula for the indicator is as follows:

$$\frac{HOUSES}{STOCKS} + 6\,(19\underline{\quad} - 1905)$$

Houses = annual median new home price (obtainable from the National Association of Home Builders; call 202-452-0200).

Stocks = annual average of the Standard and Poors 500.

For 1977 the calculation was as follows:

$$\frac{48{,}992}{96.3} + 6\,(1977 - 1905) = 509 + 432 = 941$$

189

Index

191